HINDUISM

Beliefs & Impressions

Introduction, Sanātana Dharma, Main Beliefs…

HINDUISM
Beliefs & Impressions

Introduction, Sanātana Dharma, Main Beliefs…

By
Sadhu Vivekjivandas

Editorial Consultant
Dr Janakbhai Dave

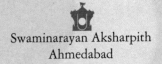

Swaminarayan Aksharpith
Ahmedabad

HINDUISM,
Beliefs & Impressions

Inspirer: HDH Pramukh Swami Maharaj

1st Edition: August 2013

Copies: 10,000

Price: ₹ 55/-

ISBN: 978-81-7526-588-2

Published & Printed by
Swaminarayan Aksharpith
Shahibaug Road, Ahmedabad-4
Gujarat, India.

Websites: www.baps.org

CONTENTS

PREFACE

"What is Sanātana Dharma or Hinduism? And what are the core beliefs that define a Hindu?

One may find it difficult to give the answers with context to the many spiritual paths and traditions that Hinduism embraces. Sanātana Dharma is the most diverse of all world religions, having thousands of different deities, sacred texts, philosophies, *sampradāyas*, mandirs, rituals, sadhanas, holy places, festivals, gurus and devotees. The multiplicity in Hinduism is bewildering to an uninformed Hindu and others. But amidst the plurality lies unity and catholicity.

The plurality in Hinduism has often been compared to a bouquet of flowers and a salad bowl. The discrete contents of a bouquet or salad bowl combine together to form a single product. Similarly, the multiplicity of beliefs, practices, *sampradāyas*, etc. all make up to produce a single, fascinating canvas called Hinduism. It has been dubbed as a "family of religions" and commonly described to be "a way of life".

The multiple beliefs and pathways to *moksha* in Sanātana Dharma reflect its freedom of worship and the choices of sadhana that suits one's innate inclinations and karmic capacities.

It is mainly because of its universality and respect for all spiritual paths that Hinduism has flourished through several millennia, and like a great river it flows tenaciously ahead, retaining the ancient while dynamically evolving to meet the present.

Hinduism, Beliefs & Impressions deals with the basic principles of Hinduism and the beliefs of a Hindu. For a Hindu unacquainted with the rudiments of Sanātana Dharma, this book will not only enlighten but also breathe meaning to the practices and beliefs he or she follows. For those curious about Hinduism the book will serve to inform and also facilitate in gaining a better understanding of Hinduism. In the introduction to the book, the reader will get a bird's-eye view of the different aspects that comprise Hinduism. The reader will come across some repetitions about certain beliefs and principles in the first two chapters, but they have been made to justify the topics. For the more interested readers references to Hindu sacred texts and of scholars are provided as footnotes. We hope this publication will motivate the readers to study and experience Hinduism further.

- Author

Hinduism is a mosaic of fascinating rituals, festivals, celebrations, sacred texts, beliefs, mandirs and practices

1. INTRODUCTION

Sanātana Dharma, commonly referred to as Hinduism, is considered by many of its believers and practitioners to be the world's oldest living dharma or religion that originated from the Indian subcontinent. It has also been described as Vaidika Dharma (religion rooted in the Vedas), Ārya Dharma (dharma of Āryans) and Mānava Dharma (religion of humanity).

Hindu traditionalists prefer to call it Sanātana Dharma. Sanātana means eternal and also ancient. And dharma in this case means religion, however, it has a much more deeper meaning than religion. So, Sanātana Dharma means the religion or the tradition of spiritual beliefs, disciplines and practices that are not only ancient but also eternal. In other words Hinduism is a tradition of spiritual, cultural and social disciplines and practices of great antiquity, with its main roots in the Vedas and continuing relevance to our own times.

Hinduism derives its name from the ancient Persians who called the River Sindhu, that flows through modern day Pakistan, as Hindu, because 'S' was pronounced as 'H' in their language. Subsequently, as a result of this linguistic practice, the people living on the eastern banks of Sindhu came to be known as Hindus, and much later the British developed the term Hinduism to describe the various religious traditions they encountered across the country. Thus the name Hindu had a geographical significance. After the Persians, the Greeks called the river Hindu (i.e. Sindhu), 'Indos', and the people, 'Indoi'. In English the words 'Indos' and 'Indoi' became Indus and Indians.

Throughout the course of history, Hinduism has been like a great river that tenaciously moves forward, retaining the ancient while dynamically evolving to meet the present.

WHAT IS HINDUISM?

Sanātana Dharma evolved over a period of several centuries, thanks to hundreds of enlightened rishis or sages. So, it does not have one founder and philosophy. It is often referred to as a family of religious traditions because of its many deities, sacred texts, philosophies, *sampradāyas* and religious leaders. This makes Sanātana Dharma fascinating and rich, yet at the same time difficult for outsiders to grasp.

Hinduism extends the boundaries of the term "religion" beyond that which is described in Western faiths. Dr S.

Radhakrishnan, the former President of India and renowned Oxford Professor of Eastern Religions and Ethics, has famously suggested that Hinduism is more than a religion; it is a way of life. Kim Knott, Head of the Department of Theology and Religious Studies at the University of Leeds, writes, "By doing so [that is by saying that Hinduism is a way of life], he [Radhakrishnan] made the point that it was not something separate from society and politics, from making money... and getting an education. And, like other modern Hindus, he suggested that the closest term to be found within Indian thought and practice was Hindu dharma, the law, order, truth, and duties of the Hindu people."[1]

Many other scholars, historians, indologists, practitioners and spiritual leaders have described Hinduism. Pramukh Swami Maharaj, a renowned Hindu leader and head of BAPS Swaminarayan Sanstha, was asked by an Indian industrialist on 6 November 1996 to explain Hinduism in two sentences. Swamiji replied in Gujarati, *"Hindu dharma mānas ne mānava banāve chhe, ane ae mānava ne moksha no mārga shikhvāde chhe."* It means, "Hindu dharma makes an individual into a civilized person, and teaches the person [to attain] the path of *moksha* [liberation]." The words of Swamiji brilliantly

---

1. Knott, Kim. *Hinduism, A Very Short Introduction.* Oxford: Oxford University Press (OUP), 2000, p. 111.

3

summarize Hinduism in brief. One finds them to be true because the basic practice of morality prescribed by the Hindu sacred texts, namely, *satya* (truth), *dayā* (compassion), ahimsa (nonviolence), *brahmacharya* (continence), *asteya* (non-stealing), *aparigraha* (non-possession) and others, transforms an individual into a civilized or noble person. And the idea of *moksha* matches with the ultimate of the four goals (dharma, *artha, kāma* and *moksha*) of human life prescribed by Hinduism.

Hinduism pervades every dimension of the social, cultural and spiritual lives of the Hindus. It is alive and vibrant today in millions of homes and mandirs in India and abroad through its festivals, rituals, spiritual gurus and traditions called *sampradāyas*.

THE ĀRYAN INVASION THEORY

There are two beliefs among scholars about the founders of Vedic civilization. One group strongly propounds that the Āryans[2] came from central Asia, invaded north-western India and established the Vedic culture. The other group says that the Āryans were the original inhabitants of India and thus there was no Āryan invasion of India. Each group argues on the basis of archaeological, linguistic, textual (Rig Vedic accounts) and other sources. However, there

---

2. The word Āryan is derived from the Sanskrit word *ārya* which means 'noble'.

is a growing consensus among scholars and researchers that the Āryan invasion and Āryan migration theories are invalid.[3] Lord Colin Renfrew (1988), a British archaeologist writes, "If one checks the dozen references in the Rigveda to the Seven Rivers, there is nothing in any of them that to me implies invasion... Despite Wheeler's comments, it is difficult to see what is particularly non-Aryan about the Indus Valley Civilization."[4] Laurie Patton, Professor of Early Indian Religions at Emory University, Atlanta, USA, notes, "First, very few, if any, archaeologists or linguists embrace the invasion theory, and have not done so for several decades."[5]

The Rig Veda says the Vedic civilization flourished in north-western India, known as the land of the Saptasindhu (seven rivers). Scholars, Jim Shaffer and Diana Liechtenstein, in their paper "South Asian Archaeology in the Indo-Aryan Controversy" write, "The excavations at Mehrgarh near Sibri, Pakistan, do demonstrate an indigenous development of agricultural food production by people living there as early as the seventh millennium BC."[6]

---

3. Poliakov, L. *The Aryan Myth*. New York: Basic Books, 1974, p.4.

4. Renfrew, Colin. *Archaeology and Language: The Puzzle of Indo-European Origins*. New York: Cambridge University Press, 1988, pp. 188-190.

5. *The Indo-Aryan Controversy, Evidence and Inference in Indian History*. Edited by Edwin F. Bryant and Laurie L. Patton. London and New York: Routledge, 2005, p. 16.

6. Ibid. p.82.

Kurma avatar of Bhagwan Vishnu

Murti-pujā: Worshipping God's image

CORE BELIEFS AND PRINCIPLES

Hinduism is fascinatingly diverse, yet it has common threads or core beliefs among its many *sampradāyas*. Though not all the core beliefs may be shared by all the *sampradāyas*, a knowledge or understanding of them will help the novice grasp the basics of Hinduism without being confused by its complexity. Hinduism advocates mainly the belief in one Supreme Reality, called Paramātmā, Parameshwara, Parabrahman, Nārāyana or Bhagwan. The majority of Hindus are not polytheists as they have been erroneously branded by many observers throughout history. Hinduism can be said to exhibit its own form of monotheism. Max Müller tried to describe this as henotheism, which means belief in and worship of one supreme God without deny-

6

ing the existence of other 'gods' or forms of the supreme God. Furthermore, Sanātana Dharma includes, among its core principles, belief in the authority of the Vedas, *avatāravāda* (principle of divine incarnation), atman (soul), karma (deed), *punarjanma* (reincarnation), *murti-pujā* (image worship),

ISKCON, Ahmedabad

A devotee performs abhisheka

guru-shishya paramparā (master-disciple tradition), ahimsa, four *purushārthas* (four goals) and *varnāshrama* (social classes and stages of life) dharma. It has also explored and elaborated upon the paths of *shreyas (moksha)* and *preyas* (sensual pleasure), bhakti, dharma, *vidhis* (dos) and *nishedhas* (don'ts), different spiritual and worldly planes and the world of ancestors *(pitru loka)*, *ruta* (cosmic order by God), *satya* (in this case, moral law), sixteen samskaras (sacraments), death, liberation, philosophies, places of pilgrimage and sacred texts.

Most Hindus also believe that God is an all-pervasive reality *(sarva vyāpaka)*, who resides in all *(antaryāmin)* — both in living and non-living things. The Ishāvāsya Upanishad proclaims this in its very first *shloka*, "Ishāvāsyam idam

Vegetarian food

*Ruta or divine cosmic order
pervades infinite universes*

sarvam, yat kincha jagatyām jagat..." It means that "God pervades in all things in the world..." Mahatma Gandhi thought very highly of this *shloka* and declared, "I have now come to the final conclusion that if all the Upanishads and all the other scriptures happened all of a sudden to be reduced to ashes, and if only the first verse in the Ishopanishad [Ishāvāsya Upanishad] were left intact in the memory of Hindus, Hinduism would live forever."[7] That is why for practising Hindus their faith in the all-pervasive power of God leads to the belief that all things are fundamentally rooted in God and not in materialism or atoms. Many Hindus endeavour to observe the ideals of ahimsa, compassion

---

7. *Teachings of Mahatma Gandhi*, 1st ed., edited by Chander, Jag Parvesh. Lahore: The Indian Printing Works, 1945, p.295.

and vegetarianism[8] because of their belief in God's pervasiveness in all living beings.

Two of the important beliefs in Hinduism are the principles of *ruta* (cosmic order by God), which essentially is the law that governs the universe and nature, and *satya* (moral law). Dharma or moral law is prescribed for all humans. It refers to the path of duty, righteousness and morality. When we follow dharma, we are in tune with both God and nature.

All Hindu *sampradāyas* emphasize the need for an ethical life as an essential prerequisite to spiritual realization. Right speech, right thought and right action are promoted by all. They commonly advocate *yama* (restraint) and *niyama* (discipline), which include *satya* (truth), *dayā* (compassion), ahimsa, *brahmacharya* (celibacy), *asteya* (non-stealing) and *aparigraha* (non-greed).

PLURALISM

An outstanding feature of Hinduism is its openness towards multiple pathways or ways of being Hindu. Out of its many traditions four are most prominent: Vaishnavism, Shaivism, Shāktism and Smārtism. They are the main constituents of Sanātana Dharma. Together, they reflect the freedom of thought and the various ways of worship

---

8. Neither historically nor in the present are all Hindus vegetarian.

Jnāna: Daily reading of sacred texts

Dhyana: Spiritual meditation

that Hinduism has generously allowed to flourish. Each Hindu aspirant believes and practises according to his or her spiritual leaning, need and karmic disposition. Every person's creed depends upon his *adhikāra* or spiritual eligibility. And it is this eligibility that determines the level and type of faith one practises. Hinduism satisfies every aspirant according to his or her spiritual inclinations, needs and merits. Thus, Sanātana Dharma is a fellowship of religious traditions. The fact that the diverse or pluralistic paths of knowledge *(jnāna)*, action (karma), dhyana (meditation) and devotion (bhakti) have formed and flourished into many *sampradāyas* demonstrates Hinduism's inherent flexibility and accommodative nature. And despite its different paths there is an underlying cohesion and common

10

purpose that has sustained Hinduism for thousands of years. The fact that Hinduism has survived many devastating foreign invasions and hegemonies reflects the inner strength of its many traditions.

Bhakti: Bathing God's murti

PART AND WHOLE

Does knowing one of the many traditions of Hinduism (mainly, Vaishnavism, Shaivism, Shaktism and Smartism) mean knowing the whole? The answer is "yes" and "no". "Yes" because all the Hindu traditions have many things in common. And "no" because each of them have their own unique beliefs and practices. Hindus believe that whichever Hindu tradition they follow is related to their emotional and mental inclinations and karmic disposition *(adhikāra)* or spiritual merits *(punya)*. As their spiritual merits increase, through an intensification of sadhanas, they realize higher spiritual levels, and ultimately attain *moksha*.

BROAD-MINDEDNESS

The sacred Hindu texts introduce and teach many uni-

Tableau of a giant nest with different birds to show the world is one family

fying and universal concepts like *"Vasudhaiva kutumbakam"*– the whole world is one family[9] and *"Yatra bhavati vishvam eka nidam"* – the whole world is one nest.[10] They also teach *"Sarve sukhinaha santu"* – let all be happy and blissful,[11] and *"Ā no bhadrāhā kratavo yantu vishvataha"* – let noble thoughts come to us from the whole universe.[12] Hindus are also free to choose the path they are most inclined to among the different Hindu *sampradāyas* in realizing Paramātmā or the Ultimate Reality. Hindus do not condemn believers of other religions. Hinduism is tolerant and respects other religions. For a Hindu, respect for other world religions is not considered to be a violation of personal faith. A true Hindu respects those with different religious beliefs, while remaining faithful to his or her own deity, shastra, guru, rituals, festivals and beliefs. For Hindus, a Hindu identity is necessary for the transmission of faith to their children.

---

9. Subhāshitam (collection of popular sayings).
10. Vājasaneya Samhitā 32.8.
11. Subhāshitam (collection of popular sayings).
12. Rig Veda 1.89.1.

TRUE PERCEPTION

Many modern scholars have shown that in the past Hinduism was criticized by colonial scholars due to their own biases and misunderstandings. Even today, when Hinduism is criticized, it might be because of the critic's incorrect perceptions or preset beliefs based upon

A true guru is one of the pillars of Hinduism

his or her own religion and culture. Imagine the difficulties one would encounter if one tried to interpret physics from the principles of biology. Hinduism can be fully perceived and experienced by a practising Hindu or a sincere scholar – if they both accept the guidance of a bona fide Hindu guru.

Such gurus, in addition to mandirs and shastras, are the main pillars of Hinduism. Hindu rituals, festivals and spiritual practices revolve mainly around and celebrate these three main aspects.

CLARIFYING HINDU VIEWS

As Hindus there is no need to change or give up one's principle beliefs in order to satisfy other religious and so-called secular viewpoints. And neither should Hindus be swayed or be left in doubt about their own principles when people or scriptures of other faiths contradict and criticize them. Some scholars and audiences have misinterpreted some of the principles or practices of Hinduism. One such misconception is that Hinduism is world-negating. Perhaps such conclusions have been derived from observations of Hindu ascetics who wander in society without possessions or personal care, perform severe austerities in remote caves and mortify their flesh. Such conclusions may also have been extrapolated from some philosophical teachings that describe the world to be false or illusory.

Hinduism, however, is not world-negating or non-compassionate, and does not teach to shun one's duty, sympathy and empathy. Renunciation and austerities are a part of spiritual sadhanas or practices, in which an aspirant or ascetic cultivates *vairāgya* or inner indifference to worldly objects and situations. This enables him to eradicate his mundane desires and realize his own atman and God.

Another point to note is that the majority of Hindus are householders leading a normal family life and fulfilling social responsibilities and duties. Furthermore, the Bhagavad Gitā advocates action and doing one's duty, and preaches that work is worship, "Do your own allotted work, (for) work is better than inaction, even the sustenance of your

14

An ascetic engaged in austerity   *A Hindu family*

body cannot be accomplished from inaction."[13] The Hindu shastras also prescribe the four *purushārthas* (endeavours or goals), namely, dharma, *artha, kāma* and *moksha*, which are the roadmap of life, prompting all to make efforts to achieve them.

At other times, Hindus have been branded to be fatalistic because of their beliefs in the karma principle (the universal law of cause and effect with regards to one's actions) and God's all-doership. As fatalistic followers, Hindus are criticized as uncompassionate to those who are suffering, physically challenged or have lost their lives in natural calamities. Hinduism, however, does not teach fatalism.

---

13. Bhagavad Gita (B.G.) 3.8.

*Hindus worship different deities, with many believing
that they revere the same supreme God*

Arvind Sharma, Birks Professor of Comparative Religion, McGill University, Canada, asserts, "To think fatalistically about karma is unhelpful when, in fact, as human beings we have the power at any moment to change our own behaviour, and thus its consequences for our future. Free will rather than fatalism characterizes the operation of karma."[14] Hinduism celebrates the karma principle as the individual's freedom to create his or her future state of existence through his or her present actions and thoughts.

Some also think that all Hindus believe in many "Gods". But this is not so. The Hindus mainly believe in one Supreme Paramātmā, who manifests in various human and other

---

14. Knott, Kim. *Hinduism – A Very Short Introduction.* Oxford: OUP, 2000, p.39.

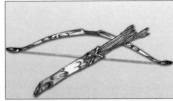

Top left, clockwise: A symbolic representation of the ancient Varna System, comprising of the Brahmins (spiritual mentors), Kshatriyas (rulers and protectors), Shudras (weavers and labourers) and Vaishyas (farmers and businessmen)

forms to reestablish faith and morality.[15] They worship only one or several of his manifestations with the belief that they are worshipping the Supreme Bhagwan.

CASTE SYSTEM

Another aspect that is severely criticised and taught in some textbooks and by some teachers is the caste system. It has been broadcast, written about and taught with such enormity and force as if Hinduism is mostly just about the caste system. But this view is greatly flawed. The caste system is believed to be an aberration of the original Varna

---

15. B.G. 4.8: "For the deliverance of the good and the destruction of the wicked and for establishing righteousness I come into being age after age."

System which was based on a person's qualities *(gunas)* and aptitude for a particular type of work (karma).[16] Some believe that over time, discrimination and class hierarchy crept in due to human imperfections and ego. Recognizing the growing rigidity and injustice of the decaying system, modern reformers of India from the 19th century onwards like Bhagwan Swaminarayan, Raja Ram Mohan Roy, Dayananda Sarasvati, Swami Vivekananda, Mahatma Gandhi and others made great efforts to eradicate discrimination based on caste.

Every society has its problems and issues. Many Hindus have recognized their problems and have taken steps at many levels to rectify them. Although sati, dowry and caste discrimination continue to exist in some places, they are officially banned by the Indian Penal Code.[17] Many Hindu and social organizations have been making active efforts to eradicate these inequities. The rapid urbanization and spread of education in India in the last century has also mitigated caste discrimination. But there are those who believe in the caste system for several reasons; one of which is to ensure their idea of an ideal or compatible marriage.

---

16. Ibid. 4.13 *(varnas)*. "According to the differentiation of *guna* and karma, the four divisions of human society are created by Me."

17. Prohibition of Sati Act (1829), Untouchability Offences Act (1955) and Dowry Prohibition Act (1961).

SCIENCE AND LITERATURE

For many Hindus, religion and science, faith and rationality are not viewed as incompatible. In Hinduism, spirituality does not reject reason, and reasoning does not deny faith. Sages like Sushruta, Charaka, Āryabhatta, Varāhamihira, Nāgārjuna and others made pioneering discoveries and inventions in science. They established some of the most popular sciences like ayurveda, yoga, *sthāpatya* shastra (science of architecture), *artha* shastra (science of economics), mathematics, astronomy, surgery, etc.

Remains of Nālandā – an ancient Indian university, now in Bihar, India

Vladimir K

India is also the land where great works of literature and epics like the Rāmāyana, Mahābhārata and others were written by enlightened rishis. Great rishis and teachers taught in Takshashilā (c. 500 BCE) and Nālandā (500-1300 CE), India's premier universities, to over 10,000 students from India and abroad in about 68 different branches of knowledge. The Indian rishis and masters endeavoured in nearly all domains of spiritual and secular knowledge to understand the universe, life, soul and God in a holistic way.

19

ANCIENT CIVILIZATION, MODERN RELEVANCE

As the ancient Hindus ventured abroad and outsiders visited India, there was a natural transmission of the vast knowledge, wisdom, traditions, practices and experiences of Hinduism.

Today, Hinduism is a representative of not only India but the ancient wisdom of humanity. In our age of globalization, the scourges of fanaticism, terrorism, sectarian violence, exploitation of human beings and the environment, and a plethora of social and moral ills are ever burgeoning and causing untold damage, anxieties and dismay. The inspiring values of Hinduism effect a positive change and provide lasting solutions to our growing conflicts and problems.

Dr Arnold J. Toynbee (1889-1975), the noted British historian, expressed, "It is already becoming clear that a chapter which had a Western beginning, will have to have an Indian ending, if it is not to end in self-destruction of the human race. At this supremely dangerous moment in human history, the only way of salvation is the ancient Hindu way."[18]

After reading the Bhagavad Gītā, Ralph Waldo Emerson, (1803-1882), Lecturer in Theology at Harvard University and a Unitarian minister, wrote, "I owed a magnificent day to the *Bhagavat Geeta*. It was the first of books; it was as if an empire spake to us, nothing small or unworthy, but large, serene, consistent, the voice of an old intelligence which in

---

18. Toynbee, Arnold. J. *A Study of History,* published in 12 volumes.

Dr Arnold J. Toynbee   Ralph Waldo Emerson

another age and climate had pondered and thus disposed of the same questions which exercise us."[19]

Sanātana Dharma is basically a holistic religion that inspires morality, faith, peace, love, service to God and mankind. Hence, it has the capacity to nourish and liberate people of different spiritual inclinations and natures, and provide valid answers to individual problems and global crises. The more one learns about and experiences Hinduism, the more one comes to appreciate its richness, depth, comprehensive approach, celebratory spirit, magnanimity and capacity to relieve people from all types of bondage and suffering and elevate their souls to the height of eternal joy and happiness.

19. *Journals of Ralph Waldo Emerson,* Vol.7, edited by Edward Waldo Emerson and Waldo Emerson Forbes. London: Constable & Co. Ltd., and Boston and New York: Houghton Mifflin Company, 1913, p.511.

The magnificent Himalayas have spiritual vibrations because of the austerities of hundreds of ancient rishis and the divine revelations graced upon them by Paramātmā.

2. SANĀTANA DHARMA

INTRODUCTION

In ancient times the Hindus were known as Āryas[1] (meaning the 'noble' ones). The Āryas called their religion[2] the 'Ārya Dharma' – 'Religion of the Āryas'. Later, it was also known as 'Mānava Dharma' – the religion of humankind based on human values; 'Sanātana Dharma' – 'The Eternal Religion'; and 'Vaidika Dharma' – the religion rooted in the Vedas.

The term Hinduism was unknown to the ancient Āryas or Āryans. It came much later and much after the Persians coined the word Hindu. Persia (now Iran) had a common border with ancient India or Āryāvarta[3] – the land of the Āryans. The common border was the River Sindhu (called Indus in English) that runs down from the north in the Himalayas. The ancient Persians pronounced 'S' as 'H' and thus Sindhu became Hindu. And they named the Āryans, living on the eastern side of the River Sindhu, Hindus. Several

---

1. The English distortion of the Sanskrit word Ārya is Āryan.
2. Note: The meaning of the term 'religion' is dharma in the context of Hinduism. For meaning of dharma see pp.17-18.
3 Ancient India was also known as Brahmarshidesha, Brahmāvarta, Madhyadesha, Jambudvipa and Bhāratavarsha.

Guru teaching the Vedic mantras in a gurukula

millennia later the religion of the Āryans became known as Hinduism, the term first used by orientalist scholars in the early nineteenth century, and the entire country came to be called Hindustan (the land of the Hindus). Taking the cue from the Persians, the Greeks called the Sindhu as 'Indos' and the people as 'Indoi', and later in English the river came to be known as 'Indus' and the people 'Indian'.

In the Rig Veda, the Indian sub-continent or Bhārata, as it was popularly known later, is called the region of Saptasindhu, i.e. the land of the seven great rivers.[4]

DIVINE REVELATION

Sanātana Dharma was not founded by any mortal person.

---

4. Seven great rivers: Sarasvati (Sarsuti), Sindhu, Vitasta (Jhelum), Parushni (Rāvi), Askini (Chenāb), Vipāsha (Beās), and Shutudri (Satlaj).

For many Hindus the Supreme Reality or Paramātmā revealed the spiritual truths to different enlightened sages or rishis while they were in a state of samadhi.[5] The sages then transmitted this wisdom to their disciples through recitations.[6] These revealed truths are called the Shruti or Veda. Shruti means "that which is heard" or revealed. The name Veda comes from the Sanskrit root word 'vid' which means 'to know'. The Vedas or the Shruti shastras are the fundamental sacred texts of the Hindus.

The Vedas are *apaurusheya*, meaning not man-made. Since the truths were divinely revealed by God they are also eternal like God himself, hence the name Sanātana Dharma – The Eternal Dharma. Many Hindus and scholars believe that they were transmitted through the ages to the present day with very little changes. The noted Orientalist and Sanskrit scholar, A.A. Macdonell (1854-1930 CE) wrote about

5. The final state in yoga, wherein one experiences the presence and bliss of God.
6. Jean Le Mée, the author of *Hymns from the Rig-Veda,* writes, "Precious or durable materials – gold, silver, bronze, marble, onyx, or graphite – have been used by most ancient peoples in an attempt to immortalize their achievements. Not so, however, with the ancient Aryans. They turned to what may seem the most volatile and insubstantial material of all – the spoken word – and out of this bubble of air fashioned a monument which more than thirty, perhaps forty, centuries later stands untouched by time or the elements. For the Pyramids have been eroded by the desert wind, the marble broken by earthquakes, and the gold stolen by robbers, while the Vedas remains, recited daily by an unbroken chain of generations, travelling like a great wave through the living substance of the mind." Published by Jonathan Cape Ltd, London, 1975, p. ix.

the Rig Veda, "Excepting single mistakes of tradition in the first, and those due to grammatical theories in the second period,[7] the old text of the Rigveda thus shows itself to have been preserved from a very remote antiquity with marvellous accuracy even in the smallest details."[8] Hindus believe that the Vedas are the most ancient of the world's sacred texts. Even today they are regularly recited and applied in almost all sacred ceremonies in countless mandirs and homes.

Hinduism has no single author because the revelations are considered by Hindus to have been made to many rishis, none of whom claimed to be the author or sole receptor of the revelations by God.

MEANING OF SANĀTANA DHARMA

Sanātana means eternal. Dharma is often translated to mean 'religion'. The Concise Oxford English Dictionary defines religion as, "The belief in and worship of a super human controlling power, especially a personal God or gods."[9] It also includes belief in tenets and practice of rituals.

The term 'dharma', however, has a multi-layered meaning. It is derived from the Sanskrit root word *dhru*, which means

---

7. The first period refers to existence of the Rig Veda alone before the other Vedas came into being, and the second period refers to when the Rig Veda appeared in the phonetically modified form called the Samhitā text.

8. Macdonell, Arthur A. *A History of Sanskrit Literature*. New York: D. Appleton and Company, 1900, p. 48.

9. *Concise Oxford English Dictionary*. Oxford: OUP, 11th edition, 2004, p. 1215.

'to hold'. Dharma means that which 'upholds', 'supports' or 'nourishes' the existence of a thing or being. Dharma also means the essential nature or the defining characteristic of something. Everything in the universe has its dharma, because all things owe their very existence to it. For example, the dharma or essential nature of fire is its power to burn and give light and heat. The dharma or principal nature of water is its quality to wet and flow. And, for inanimate objects, they share the dharma or principle of inertness.

Man also has a core nature that sustains his existence; which is distinct from that of the rest of creation. Hindus believe that the essential dharma or nature of man is humaneness (*mānushyam*), discernment (*viveka*) and the power to become divine. Man's essential nature differentiates him from all other living things because it gives him the power to choose between right and wrong and to attain divine qualities.

Sanātana Dharma therefore means that which eternally 'supports' or 'nourishes' everyone and everything, i.e. all life and the entire creation. It is in this context that Hindus describe Sanātana Dharma or Hinduism as the 'eternal religion'. 'Dharma' in its simplest form also means truth, law, duty and obligation. Sanātana Dharma is popularly known as Hinduism.

From the perspective of the Semitic religions (Judaism, Christianity and Islam), religion is defined as having

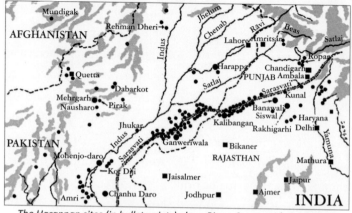

The Harappan sites (in bullet points) along Rivers Sarasvati (now extinct) and Indus (Sindhu)

one transcendent God, a sole founder, one scripture, one governing institution or church, priests and other dimensions such as a single set of tenets, ethics and rituals. From the perspective of Sanātana Dharma, religion has a much broader concept, since Sanātana Dharma believes in one Supreme Reality called Paramātmā or Bhagwan and his manifestations. It does not have a single founder or a central institution. So, Sanātana Dharma, which is treated as a religion, is a religion that has a different connotation from the Western meaning. In fact, Sanātana Dharma comprises of many *sampradāyas* or religious traditions.

HISTORY

The ancient civilization of India developed between two

great rivers – the Sindhu[10] (also known as Indus, now in Pakistan) and the Sarasvati[11] (now not visible and believed to have dried up around 1900 BCE). The Sarasvati River, once ran parallel to the Sindhu, roughly 300 km east of it.

Both the rivers are believed to have been in existence since Vedic times. The Rig Veda describes the Sarasvati[12] as a mighty river flowing from the "mountains to the sea" (Rig Veda 2.

---

10. The Sindhu or Indus River originates in the Tibetan plateau in the vicinity of Lake Mānasarovar in Tibet. Today the river travels through the Ladākh district of Jammu and Kashmir and then enters Northern Areas (Gilgit-Baltistan), flowing through the north in a southerly direction along the entire length of Pakistan, to merge into the Arabian Sea near the port city of Karachi in Sindh.

11. The Sarasvati River had originated from the Kapāla Tso (lake) in the Himalayas to the southeast of Kailāsa, and probably flowed southward to Mānasarovar. From there it is believed to have descended through Rākshashatāl, Plaksha Prasravana lake, Ādibadri (presently Dhuling Math in Tibet), Mānā Pass, Kedārnātha, Rishikesha, Haridwāra, Merut, Delhi, Mathurā, Bharatpur, between Pāli and Jodhpur and flowed up to Panchpadrā in Rajasthan. From here it entered into Gujarat and flowed through Siddhapur, Pātan and finally met the Arabian Sea near Prabhās Pātan. In its long journey, the Sarasvati is believed to have been joined by the rivers Shatadru (Satlaj) originating from Mount Kailāsa, Drishadvati from Siwālik Hills and the old Yamunā. Through the millennia the river had changed its course many times. (Thakker, P.S., Probable Course of River Vedic Sarasvati Through Remote Sensing Data. In *Rasik Bhārati*. Gandhinagar: Sanskrit Sahitya Akademi. 2005)

12. In 1978, satellite images from earth sensing satellites launched by NASA and ISRO (Indian Space Research Organization) showed traces of an ancient river course on the very route of the River Sarasvati. They clearly showed the dried bed to be six to eight kilometres wide, and at some places to be 14 kilometres, which is larger than the River Gangā today. (Source: Dr J.R. Sharma and his colleagues A.K. Gupta and G. Shreenivasan of the Remote Sensing Centre of ISRO, Jodhpur, Rajasthan, mapped the course of the once mighty River Sarasvati.)

River Indus (Sindhu) flows through mountainous terrain in Pakistan

41.16, 7.95.2).[13] Archaeological and sacred textual evidence shows that there was significant religious activity in the proto-historic (ancient) period of the Indus and Sarasvati civilizations. The Indus valley civilization developed on the River Sindhu, and Harappa and Mohenjo-daro (excavated in Pakistan) were two cities of this highly developed urban civilization. Dholavira and Lothal (in Gujarat, India) are remnants of the same civilization. H.D. Sankalia, a veteran Indian archaeologist and indologist, states, "While Mehergarh serves as an excellent preface to the rich Indus civilization, this civilization itself has now been found all over Gujarat, Kutch, Saurashtra, and seen to have crossed Madhya Pradesh and reached Maharashtra."[14]

---

13. Similar references are found in the Aitareya Brāhmana (2.19.1,2), Panchavimsa Brāhmana (25.10.7) and Shatapatha Brāhmana (7.2.1,4). The great epic Mahābhārata declares that various Vedic sacrifices were performed on the banks of this river (Ādiparva 95.26 and Vanaparva 36.41). Expert geologists, Puri and Verma, (1998) express the same view about the River Sarasvati in 'Glaciological and Geological Source of Vedic Sarasvati in the Himalayas' in *Itihāsa Darpan*, ix (2): pp. 7-36.

14. Sankalia, H.D. Down the Corridors of Indian Archaeology. In *Indian Heritage*, edited by Vasanti Mazumdar. Bombay: Indian Council of Social Welfare, 1980, p.2.

Dholavira site, Gujarat   Lothal site, Gujarat

The Vedic civilization developed on the banks of River Sarasvati; it is also known as the Sarasvati civilization, which is geographically depicted in the Rig Veda.

The Sarasvati River is mainly mentioned in literary sources, i.e. the Rig Veda, having no other proof until recently. Through Satellite imagery scientists have discovered paleo-channels (geological formations indicating an ancient dried river bed) along a path through which the Sarasvati flowed. On the other hand the Indus civilization left behind hundreds of archaeological relics like towns, ports, figures, figurines, jewellery, seals, etc. The seals found here have a script, which has remained undeciphered till this day. Therefore it is difficult to make a definite statement about their authors, cultures and time frame. But both the Indus and the Sarasvati civilizations can be seen as having contributed to the development of Hinduism.

Recent scholars have concluded that Indian culture is at least over 9,000 years old. "The excavations at Mehrgarh (Jansen et al. 1991; Jarrige et al. 1995) near Sibri, Pakistan, do demonstrate an indigenous development of agricultural food production by people living there as early as the seventh millennium BC. As a cultural occupation, Mehrgarh Period 1A[15] dates to the seventh millennium BC period (Shaffer 1992); because of the essential cultural complexity in that occupation stratum, some scholars posit an even earlier period for the cultural innovation there of achieving plant and animal domesticates."[16]

The discovery of some vestiges of the Indus valley civilization occurred by accident. When two British engineers who were in charge of constructing a railway line had the mounds at Harappa dug, they discovered burnt bricks which could be used as ballast. Little did they know that they were digging up a past and hitherto unknown facet of the history of India! The bricks turned out to be more than 4,000 years old! After this initial discovery and excavation, large scale excavations were carried out by British

---

15. Period 1A indicates the first excavation at Mehrgarh. The second excavation is noted as 1B, and so on.

16. Shaffer, Jim G. and Lichenstein, Diane A. South Asian Archaeology and the Myth of Indo-Aryan Invasions. In *The Indo-Aryan Controversy*, edited by Bryant and Patton. London: Routledge, 2005, p. 82.

and Indian archaeologists, Sir John Marshall and E.J.H. Mackay at Mohenjo-daro and M.S. Vatsa at Harappa in 1921-22. These two highly advanced cities were discovered to be about 600 km apart.

Ruins of Mohenjo-daro, 300 km north of Hyderabad (Sindh), Pakistan

The society and culture of these cities are referred to as the Indus valley civilization or the Harappan civilization. Some other important sites of this civilization are Kalibangan in Rajasthan, and Dholavira, Lothal and Rangpur in Gujarat, India.

From the evidence found[17] it has been proved that India had a highly advanced civilization in other areas of the sub-continent. Several hundreds of towns and sites existed near

---

17. Recently, divers of the National Institute of Ocean Technology (NIOT) have discovered an ancient city submerged in the gulf of Khambhāt (Cambay) in Gujarat. Sonar mapping of the site revealed it to be 10km by 2km, or the size of Manhattan. Radiocarbon dating of a wooden object from the site showed it to be 7500 BCE. Glenn Milne of the University of Durham, using inundation maps and sea level curves estimates that the city may have been submerged 10,000 or even 12,000 years ago. Considering that it is vast and sophisticated, a long period of development must have preceded it. This means the urban culture to which it belonged must have been much older. Source: Gupta, H.K. (2002) Oldest Neolithic settlements discovered in Gulf of Cambay. *Journal* of the Geological Society of India, v.59(3), pp.277-278.

The 'Great Bath' at Mohenjo-daro

the banks of the Sindhu and Sarasvati Rivers and other neighbouring regions.

FACTS AND ARTEFACTS OF INDUS CIVILIZATION

The well-planned cities of Harappa, Mohenjo-da-ro and others of the Indus civilization had two-storey houses of brick and stone, large community baths, properly planned drainage and sewage systems, and well-built roads, which in some places were sixty-feet wide. Wood was generously used, not only for construction purposes, but also for making a variety of furniture like cots, chairs, stools and tables. Its people cultivated wheat, barley and dates; domesticated animals from the camel to the humped zebu; and had invented the wheel and yoked buffalo or oxen to their carts. They used gold, silver, lead, tin, copper, bronze and garments of spun and woven cotton more than 3,000 years ago.

One of the most noteworthy features of Harappa was its big granaries. There were twelve granaries arranged in two parallel rows, with ventilation and passages of approach. The distinctive feature of Mohenjo-daro was "the great

Bath". It was built of brick set in gypsum mortar with a damp-proof layer of bitumen. The bath is 54 by 33 metres (177 by 108 ft). The outer walls are 2 to 2.5 metres (7 to 8 ft) in thickness. In the centre of the paved quadrangle is a large swimming bath, 11 by 7 metres (39 by 23 ft).

Let us consider some common aspects typical to all the sites of the Indus Civilization. "People were mostly vegetarians and ate fish also. Apart from wheat, barley and rice they also grew fruits and vegetables like pumpkin, dates and coconuts. The ornaments they used were girdles, earrings, bangles, necklaces, nose-rings, anklets, hairpins and beads. Weights and measures had been standardized. Trade and commerce by land and by sea with Sumeria, Babylonia and Egypt were flourishing. People were good at arts and crafts. Music and dancing were also known to them, as can be guessed through figures found on seals. Worship of Shiva-Pashupati, goddess Durgā, *lingas* and certain animals and trees like bison, fish, serpent, tulsi and peepal tree seem to have existed."[18]

Many of the artefacts and relics found from these cities include seals, statues, female figurines, beads, pottery, tools, jewellery, games and children's toys such as small carts. More than 3,000 seals and artefacts have been found so far.

---

18. Swami Harshananda. *A Concise Encylopaedia of Hinduism,* Vol. 2. Bangalore: Ramakrishna Math, 2008, pp. 70-71.

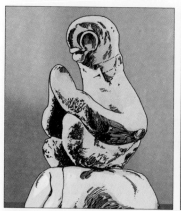 

Left: An illustration of a male terracotta figurine offering namaste, Harappa
Right: An illustration of a female terracotta figure testifies to the use of vermilion in circa 2800-2600 BCE, Harappa.

Some of the symbols and illustrations are *swastika*-like figures (symbol of auspiciousness and good fortune), a one-horned animal (that probably represents the Varāha avatar of Bhagwan Vishnu), objects similar to Shiva *lingas*, figures in dancing poses, and the most discussed of all the Harappan seals depicting a deity in a yogic posture surrounded by animals is believed to be Bhagwan Shiva called Pashupati – the Lord of Animals. The inscriptions on the seals have still remained elusive to experts who are unable to decipher their script. But the symbols and illustrations reflect distinct highly developed and planned urban civilization of the Indus valley.

A Harappan seal: The so-called unicorn bull, believed to represent the Varaha avatar (divine boar)

A Harappan seal: A three-headed figure in a yogic posture. It is identified to be Bhagwan Shiva as Pashupati

THE ĀRYAN INVASION THEORY

As mentioned earlier in the 'Introduction', there are two hotly argued views among scholars about the Āryan invasion of or migration to India. This controversial topic is not intended to distract readers from learning about Hinduism. Rather, bringing up this issue about the history of ancient India is to provide some historical context for the texts and traditions that are the primary focus of this introductory book. The following text explains briefly about the two theories. The case for the invasion/migration theories will be understood from the arguments given against the Āryan invasion theory.

But first, let us briefly understand what the Āryan

Countries of Central Asia (circled) from where the Aryans are believed to have come to India, according to some Western scholars

invasion theory is. Many scholars and books of Indian history teach about the Āryan invasion of India, describing that the Āryans were people who came from Central Asia or Europe. According to these scholars they invaded India around 1500 BCE. After overpowering and killing some of the inhabitants of the Indus valley who had built the cities of Harappa and Mohenjo-daro, they established themselves over north India. They are said to have composed the Rig Veda and other Vedic literature and founded the Vedic civilization.

Max Müller, an Oxford University scholar and German-born Indologist of the 19th century, strongly propagated the Āryan Invasion theory and announced that the Vedas were composed in 1200 BCE. Prof. B. B. Lal, former Director

General of ASI and former Head of the School of Studies in Ancient Indian History at Jivaji University, Gwalior, in his chapter *Āryan Invasion of India – Perpetuation of a Myth*[19], argues that Müller arbitrarily assigned the Vedas to have been composed in 1200 BCE. B.B. Lal says that Max Müller

German-born Indologist, Max Müller

accepted the time of Buddha, i.e. 600 to 500 BCE, and then he gave a period of 200 years to each of the successively preceding periods of Vedic literature, namely, Āranyakas, Brāhmanas and Vedas. When, however, he was criticized by a host of his contemporaries such as Theodor Goldstucker (1821-1872, a German Sanskrit scholar), William D. Whitney (1827-1894, an American linguist and philologist) and H.H. Wilson (1786-1860, an English orientalist), Müller admitted that he had hypothetically assigned 200 years to each period of Vedic literature. Prof. B.B. Lal quotes Max Müller, "All I have claimed for them has been that they are minimum dates, and that the literary productions of each

19. *The Indo-Aryan Invasion Controversy.* Edited by Bryant and Patton. London: Routledge, 2005, pp. 50-51.

period which either still exists or which formerly existed could hardly be accounted for within shorter limits of time than those suggested...

"If now we ask as to how we can fix the dates of these periods, it is quite clear that we cannot hope to fix a *terminun a qua {sic}*. Whether the Vedic hymns were composed [in] 1000 or 2000 or 3000 years BC, no power on earth will ever determine."[20] Later in life, Max Müller had second thoughts about his estimate on the date of the Vedas and admitted, "Whatever may be the date of the Vedic hymns, whether 1500 or 15000 BC, they have their own unique place and stand by themselves in the literature of the world."[21]

The descriptions in the Vedas, archaeological excavations and other scientific facts also prove otherwise. Some of the arguments as to why the Āryan invasion never happened are as follows:[22]

❖ There is no memory of an invasion or of a large-scale migration in the records of ancient India – neither in the Vedas, in Buddhist or Jain records, nor in Tamil literature.

❖ The Rig Veda describes the landscape, fauna, flora and

20. Müller, Max. *Physical Religion*. New Delhi: Asian Educational Services, 1890 (1979), p. 51.
21. Müller, Max. *The Six Systems of Philosophy*. Reprint Varanasi: Chowkhamba, 1962, p.35.
22. Klostermaier, K.K. *Hinduism, A Short History*. Oxford: One World, 2000, pp.37-39.

Illustrations of vessels of clay relics from Mehrgarh

climate of northern India, but does not mention the countryside in the Caucasus near the Caspian Sea or other parts of Central Asia that some Western scholars assert as the original home of the Āryans.

❖ There is cultural continuity between the archaeological findings of the Indus-Sarasvati civilization and subsequent Indian society and culture: a continuity of religious ideas, arts, crafts, architecture, and system of weights and measures. If there was an Āryan invasion then there would not have been a cultural continuity.

❖ The archaeological discoveries of relics at Mehrgarh reveal a culture similar to that of the Vedic Indians. The Rig Veda shows not a nomadic but an urban culture. The supposed Āryans who invaded India and wrote the

Vedas had a nomadic culture.

* The racial diversity found in skeletons in cities of the Indus civilization is the same as in today's India; there is no evidence of a new race from outside India.

* The Indus cities were not destroyed by invaders but deserted by their inhabitants because of desertification of the area due to the change in course of River Sindhu or Indus. Strabo, a Greek historian, reports (Geography xv.1.19) that Aristobulas had seen hundreds of villages and towns deserted because the Indus had changed its course.

* The battles described in the Rig Veda were not fought between invaders and natives but between people belonging to the same culture.

* Archaeologically there are no ruins, remains, or settlements of any invading Āryans that existed apart from the indigenous developments.

* The Āryan invasion theory was based on the assumption that a nomadic people (the supposed Āryans from abroad) possessing horses and chariots defeated an urban civilization (the Indus or Harappa civilization) that is believed to not have had any horses. And in the Rig Veda horses are described to be of great importance, both as secular and sacred objects. This supposedly proves that there was an Āryan invasion. But archaeological

evidence demonstrates that the Harappan knew the use of horses. Horse teeth have been found in Amri on the Indus and Rana Ghundai on the Baluchistan border which is dated to 3600 BCE. Bones of the domesticated horse have been found in early layers of excavations in

An illustration of Mortimer Wheeler who advocated the Āryan invasion theory

Harappa, so this precludes the possibility that they were left by the 'invaders'.

From 1944 to 1946, Mortimer Wheeler, Director General of ASI, worked on excavating the Indus Valley sites. He strongly advocated the Āryan invasion from the skeletal remains he found at Mohenjo-daro. His account is found in history textbooks.[23] But, later archaeologists disproved Wheeler's interpretation with the fact that the skeletons showed no evidence of violent deaths and no Harappan sites have been found to be destroyed by outside invaders. There are, to date, no ruins, remains of encampments or

---

23. *The Indus Civilization: Cambridge History of India.* Cambridge University Press, 1953, p.92.

settlements and relics clearly indicating any invading Āryans apart from indigenous developments.

Prof. B.B. Lal, former student of Mortimer Wheeler, argues against his mentor's theory, saying that, "There is no evidence of attacks on the citadels of the Harappan cities, which would have been the first structures to be destroyed in the case of an attack." Further, Lal adds that the thirty-seven skeletal remains are from a lower level of the site. If these skeletons did really represent the massacre by invaders, then they should have been on the uppermost level of the site. And lastly some vestiges of the invaders would have been found, but that is not the case. Professor of Archaeology at University of California Berkeley, George F. Dales (1964) very aptly described this so-called massacre as "The Mythical Massacre at Mohenjo-daro."[24] At the end of the introduction in *The Indo-Āryan Controversy* (2005: pp. 16-17), Ms. Laurie Patton, joint editor and professor of Early Indian Religions, writes, "Very few, if any archaeologists or linguists embrace the invasion theory and have not done so for several decades."

In recent years, with the near collapse of the Āryan Invasion Theory, some scholars have proposed the Āryan Migration Theory – the Āryans migrated to India instead

---

24. Lal, B.B. Aryan Invasion of India – Perpetuation of a Myth. In *The Indo-Aryan Controversy,* edited by Bryant and Patton. London: Routledge, 2005, pp.52-53.

of having invaded it. This theory has also become a hotly debated issue. Prof. J.G. Shaffer, a renowned archaeologist, says that modern archaeological evidence of artefacts found in Harappa and Mohenjo-daro do not support the idea of Āryan migration into India. He says, "It is possible to document archaeologically a series of cultural changes reflecting indigenous cultural development from prehistoric to historic periods."[25]

CONCLUSION

Many Hindu practioners and scholars believe that Sanātana Dharma or Hinduism is the oldest, non-proselytising religion. It is practised today by over 800 million Hindus in India and 20 million Hindus abroad.

With its holistic views and catholicity of approach, Hinduism expands the narrow boundaries of the term 'religion'. It is a mosaic of different *sampradāyas* or faiths, each adding new colour to the original. Hinduism is both very simple, i.e. a devotee can please God with a single leaf, a flower, a fruit or water as explained in the Bhagavad Gītā 9.26, and very elaborate, i.e. a royal sacrifice or Rājasuya *yajna* is recorded to have lasted for months, if not years. It touches the life of a Hindu before birth (*garbhādhān*

---

25. Cited by Flood, Gavin. *An Introduction to Hinduism.* New Delhi: Cambridge University Press, Foundation Books, First South Asian Edition, 2004, p. 33.

Jnāna-mārga: Reading a spiritual text   *Bhakti-mārga: Devotional rituals*

samskara) and is carried on even after his death *(antyeshti)*. The great philosopher and President of India, Dr S. Radhakrishnan (1888-1975), calls Hinduism a way of life with defining rules of dos and don'ts. At the same time, it gives options to reach the highest Hindu goal of life, namely, *moksha* (liberation of soul). A person may follow the paths of knowledge (*jnāna-mārga*), devotion (bhakti-*mārga*), action (karma-yoga) or dhyana-yoga (meditation) in accordance to his or her aptitude and interest. This democratic approach in matters of faith and practice is truly a distinctive feature of Hinduism. For many Hindus it is reflected in the belief in one Supreme Reality or God who is described and worshipped in many ways. It is also reflected in its tolerance and respect for people who subscribe to other belief systems.

Karma-yoga: Service to society

Dhyana-yoga: Meditation

There have been almost no organized attempts of conversion to Hinduism by inducement or force.

Hinduism's history is rich, varied and stretches back to several millennia. It is surprising that many ordinary and educated Hindus are ill-informed or ignorant of the basic tenets and traditions of their wonderful religion. The following chapter will explore some of the prominent Hindu beliefs held by one-sixth of humanity.

SUMMARY

1. The ancient Persians called people living by the eastern side of the River Sindhu as Hindu.

2. Greeks called the River Sindhu as 'Indos', and later in English it became 'Indus'. Subsequently, the country

and its people came to be known as 'India' and 'Indians' respectively.

3. Hindus were originally known as Āryas. Their religion was called Ārya Dharma, Mānava Dharma, Sanātana Dharma, Vaidika Dharma, and today, Hinduism.

4. Sanātana Dharma was revealed by God to rishis. The Vedas are called Shrutis because they were revealed by God to the rishis. They then orally transmitted them to their students.

5. Many Hindus believe that the Vedas are the most ancient sacred texts in the world, which are recited even today. The name is derived from the Sanskrit root word 'vid', which means 'to know'.

6. The civilization that developed along the banks of the Rivers Sindhu and Sarasvati came to be known as the Sindhu (Indus) and Sarasvati civilization. The River Sarasvati was roughly 300 km east of Sindhu.

7. The advanced cities of Harappa and Mohenjo-daro of the Indus Valley civilization were discovered in 1921 and 1922 respectively. They had broad roads, sewage and drainage systems, two-storey houses, seals with the *swastika*, and illustrations believed to be of Shiva in yogic posture and others.

8. Max Müller propounded the Āryan Invasion theory in 1890, saying that the Vedas were written in 1200 BCE. In

1944, Mortimer Wheeler interpreted an Āryan invasion from the skeletons found at Harappan sites. But many scholars have argued against the Invasion Theory with archaeological and sacred Hindu textual evidences. Still, the issue is being hotly debated by both sides.

Mandir, bell and lotus are important elements of Hindu tradition

3. CORE BELIEFS OF HINDUS

INTRODUCTION

What defines a Hindu? One who is born in Bharat (India) is a geographical definition of a Hindu. One who is born to Hindu parents is a familial statement. And one who is born into the fourfold caste system is a genetic inheritance description.

All these are partial definitions, because a Hindu born abroad is also a Hindu, so is a foreigner who accepts Hinduism and also one born outside the fourfold caste system. The traditional defining principles of most Hindus are the belief and faith in one Supreme Divine Reality or Paramātmā and the acceptance of the authority and infallibility of the Vedas.

While Hinduism is famously diverse, it also has common threads, or core beliefs, that are generally accepted by many of its practitioners. Exploring such prominent beliefs can help us get a clearer picture of the basic elements of Hinduism. These core Hindu beliefs generally include the principles of:

1. **One Supreme Divine Reality:** The Supreme Divine Reality or Paramātmā manifests in various forms. The Rig Veda says, *"Ekam sat viprāhā bahudhā vadanti,"*

which means "Truth is one, but the wise describe it in many ways."[1] The belief in one supreme God is called *Ekeshwaravāda*.

2. **The Authority of the Vedas:** The Vedas are the ancient shastras revealed by Paramātmā or Bhagwan to the enlightened rishis of India. They include the four Vedas (Samhitās) and their respective appendices, namely, Brāhmana, Āranyaka and Upanishad texts. The scholar Bryan K. Smith in *Reflections on Remembrance, Rituals, and Religions* (1989), writes, "Hindus are those who use the Veda as a reference point for creation, maintenance and transformation of their traditions."[2] For many Hindus the Veda is a divine revelation, and as such, its principles have not originated at a particular time in history but are eternal and of divine origin.

3. **Avatāravāda:** The principle that Bhagwan or God himself takes birth on earth in human and other forms. Avatar means "descent of God", i.e. he manifests on earth. He comes to liberate his devotees, establish dharma and destroy evil.[3]

4. **Atman:** It is unborn, eternal and indestructible inner self[4] that is the essence of life in all animate things. The

---

1. Rig Veda 1.164.45.
2. OUP, 1989, p.13.
3. B.G. 4. 7-8.
4. Ibid. 2.20.

atman is *sat* (eternal), *chitta* (consciousness) and *ānanda* (bliss). The nearest English word for atman is soul or self. The Supreme Bhagwan is believed to reside in all atmans as *antaryāmin,* inner-controller and guide.

5. **Karma:** The universal law of cause and effect according to which a person is responsible for his or her actions and their effects. God gives the appropriate fruits of a person's good or bad actions.

6. **Punarjanma:** The principle of reincarnation or rebirth (*punarjanma*)[5] in which the atman (soul) passes through many births to attain spiritual enlightenment or *moksha.* *Punarjanma* is linked to the karma principle.

7. **Murti-pujā:** A belief that God manifests in a *murti* (image) through which he can be worshipped and adored through acts of devotion. This tradition believes that God has a form, and the worship of God's *murti* is essential for spiritual elevation of the self.

8. **Guru-shishya Paramparā:** This tradition is very significant for the majority of Hindus. Through the God-realized living guru the disciple realizes the highest spiritual wisdom and attains *moksha.* A *sampradāya* is defined as *guru-shishya* tradition – "*Sampradāyaha Guru Kramaha.*"[6] This means, "Succession of gurus is called a *sampradāya.*"

5. Ibid. 4.5.

6. *Halāyudha* Dictionary, Bhumikānda. p. 402. And, Monier Williams. *A Sanskrit-English Dictionary.* Oxford: Clarendon Press, 1988, p.1,175.

9. **Four Purushārthas**: Hindu sacred texts state that there are four *purushārthas* or endeavours or goals of life, namely, dharma (staying faithful to one's moral duties), *artha* (acquiring wealth), *kāma* (fulfilling one's desires) and *moksha* (acquiring final liberation). The ultimate goal of life is *moksha* – freedom from the cycle of births and deaths through self-realization and God-realization. Out of the four *purushārthas, artha* and *kāma* are relevant for householder devotees and dharma and *moksha* are relevant for both householders and ascetics.

10. **Ahimsa**: Hindus believe that God pervades all living and non-living things. This means that God pervades humans, animals, plants, mountains and the whole of creation. Hence, the Hindus love and respect all life forms and generally practise ahimsa or nonviolence.

11. **Varnāshrama Dharma**: Dharma is generally explained as *varnāshrama* dharma. This means the duties and responsibilities of Hindus in relation to their varnas (classes) and ashramas (stages of life). Note that the varna system is not the same as the Indian caste system. The Indian caste system is a distortion of the varna system, as the caste system is purely based on one's birth. The *varnāshrama* system provided Hindu society with an organized social structure for the development and elevation of society and individuals.

Besides these eleven core beliefs there are others to which some Hindus give importance and subscribe to. Furthermore, as long as Hindus accept the belief in one supreme God and the authority of the Vedas, even if they reject some of the other core beliefs, they can still traditionally be considered Hindus. For example, certain Hindus believe that God has a form and thus they practice *murti-pujā,* while at the same time, others believe God to be formless and thus do not perform *murti-pujā.* Despite such differences, both are considered to be Hindus.

DETAILS OF EACH BELIEF

We shall now try to understand in some detail each of the eleven core beliefs that generally qualify a Hindu.

1. ONE SUPREME BHAGWAN OR GOD

Hinduism has often been misinterpreted as a religion of innumerable 'Gods'. Many Hindus believe in one Supreme Paramātmā or Bhagwan (God) who manifests in many forms. The Rig Veda clearly states *"Ekam sat viprāhā bahudhā vadanti"* – "Truth is one, but the wise describe it in many ways." Bhagwan is *sat-chit-ānanda* (eternal, consciousness and bliss). He is supreme, all-powerful, the all-doer and all-pervading. Bhagwan is the giver of the fruits of karmas to all souls (karma *phala pradātā*). He is also known as

Narayanprasad Swami

An artist's impression of the Divine who is both immanent in and transcendent to the infinite universes

Parabrahman, Paramātmā, Parmeshwara and by other names.

Bhagwan has a divine, personal form *(sākāra)*, however he is also believed by a section of Hindus to be formless or impersonal *(nirākāra)*. He comes on earth in human and other forms to liberate the pious souls, fulfil their devotional wishes and faith, and to destroy evil.[7] According to different Hindu Vaishnava traditions there have been 39 or 24 avatars (incarnations) of Bhagwan, out of which 10 (Dashāvatāra) are revered as the principal avatars. In the Shaiva and Shākta traditions there have been ten avatars in each. It is because of the many manifestations and forms of God in Hinduism that others have come to believe it to be polytheistic. But

---

7. B.G. 4.7-8.

One of many minor gods: Indra, the rain-god

Varuna, the ocean-god

principally many Hindus believe that the different forms of God are manifestations of the one Supreme Bhagwan. He possesses infinite divine qualities, out of which six are prominent: *jnāna* (knowledge), *aishwarya* (lordship), *shakti* (ability), *virya* (power), *teja* (brilliance) and *bala* (strength).

Many Hindus, especially the Vaishnavas, believe that understanding the glory of Bhagwan and worshipping him with the belief and faith that he is supreme *(sarvopari)*, the all-doer *(sarva kartā)*, always having a divine form *(divya sākāra)* and is ever present *(prakat)* on earth through a God-realized guru, liberates one from the bondage of *māyā* and blesses one with *moksha*.

Devas or *devatās* are the minor gods (namely, Indra, Agni, Surya, Varuna, Vāyu, Yama and many others), of whom there are 330 million according to the Purānas. They are all minor deities who do their duties in accordance with the authority and instructions of the supreme God.

With regard to the common features of Bhagwan in all Vaishnava *sampradāyas,* Gavin Flood, Professor of Hindu Studies and Comparative Religion, Oxford University, explains, "The Lord is the 'Supreme Person' *(Purushottama)* with personal qualities *(saguna)*, rather than an abstract absolute *(nirguna)*; the Lord is the cause of the cosmos, he creates, maintains and destroys it; the Lord reveals himself through sacred scriptures, temple icons, in his incarnations (avatar) and in saints."[8]

2. AUTHORITY OF THE VEDAS

Spiritual faith cannot be wholly imbibed in one's life in a matter of days or a couple of years. It requires a lifetime or even many lifetimes of sadhana or spiritual endeavours. But the important question is: What is required to develop absolute faith in God? How should one exert oneself? What are the pitfalls and dangers that one should be aware of? What are the practices or sadhanas required to consolidate one's faith? Is there one path or are there many? Should one follow or believe what one's mind says or take the word of any person?

---

8. *An Introduction to Hinduism.* 2004, p.118.

The Vedas are the ancient sacred texts of the Hindus.
Veda Vyāsa compiled them into four texts

The answer is that one should not follow any non-standard means or unauthorized ways. Following an authorized shastra or the bona fide guru is the Hindu tradition. The Vedas are the ancient sacred texts of the Hindus. For Hindus there is no higher scriptural authority than the Vedas. All orthodox Hindu texts derive their source and authority from the Vedas.

The orthodox Hindu schools of philosophy and *sampradāyas* are called *āstikas*,[9] mainly because they base their beliefs and practices on the Vedas, Brāhmana, Āranyaka and Upanishads. This gives them spiritual legitimacy and provides cohesion to sustain their schools

---

9. Astika schools of philosophy are Sānkhya, Yoga, Nyāya, Vaisheshika, Uttar Mimānsā and Purva Mimānsā.

of philosophy and religious traditions. Those who do not accept the Vedas are generally termed as *nāstikas* or non-believers.

3. Avatāravāda

Avatāravāda is the principle that God assumes a human or other forms to liberate countless *jivas* from material bondage and the cycle of births and deaths. It is of prime importance in Hinduism. Avatar literally means 'one who descends.' The term incarnation, is considered to be an English equivalent of avatar. However, it fails to capture the exact meaning of avatar, i.e. the belief by many Hindus that God is totally divine, despite him assuming a living form and exhibiting all the traits of a living being. Even though in a human or any other form his hunger, thirst, sleeping, eating and all other actions appear similar to humans or other living beings, yet they are divine. God's body and his actions are therefore absolutely divine and liberating.

The doctrine of *avatāravāda* or incarnation is an important feature of the Bhagavad Gitā (B.G. 4. 5-8). Some of the ten main avatars (Dashāvatāra)[10] of the Purānas

---

10. The ten avatars (Dashāvatāra): (1) Matsya (fish), (2) Kurma (tortoise), (3) Varāha (boar), (4) Nrusimha (man-lion), (5) Vāmana (dwarf), (6) Parshurāma, (7) Rāma, (8) Krishna, (9) Buddha and (10) Kalki (will ride on a white horse – yet to manifest).

are mentioned in the Vedic literature. For example, the Shatapatha Brāhmana[11] mentions the descent of God as Matsya (fish) and its story of liberation in 1.8.1.1-16, Kurma (tortoise) in 1.8.5.15, Varāha (boar) 14.1.2.1-11 and Vāmana (dwarf) 1.2.5.1.

Shri Rāma and Krishna are worshipped by many Hindus as avatars of Bhagwan Vishnu

One may ask as to why God should assume an avatar? Can he not liberate souls from his divine abode with his infinite powers? Yes he can, but the two main reasons why he incarnates in a human and other forms are: (1) To fulfil the wishes and accept the love and devotion of his devotees and countless other spiritually inclined souls, and (2) to destroy *adharma* or evil on earth.[12] The first reason allows devotees to develop deep bonds of love and glory through their personal association with God. Eventually this deep love or attachment to God liberates them from the trammels of *māyā*.

---

11. The biggest of all Brāhmana texts. It belongs to the Shukla Yajur Veda. The work, almost entirely, deals with various aspects of Vedic *yajnas*.

12. *"Yadā yadā hi dharmasya..."* B.G. 4. 7-8.

4. ATMAN OR JIVA

The nearest translation of atman or *jiva* is self or soul. Hindus believe that all living things have a *jiva* or atman. It is the fundamental principle of all life which pervades the body and experiences.

The ancient rishis of India turned their thoughts inward to discover their inner self. They had a unique experience of a metaphysical entity, i.e. self, that was beyond the external, physical world they were living in. They found it to be eternally existing *(sat)*, having consciousness *(chit)* and infinitely blissful *(ānanda)*. This self is luminous, pure and bodiless; beyond sorrow and decay. The rishis discovered that what they experienced was their true self and the very essence of their life. They called it atman or *jiva* or *jivātmā*, which is pure, immortal and untouched by evil. The Bhagavad Gitā describes the nature of atman in chapter 2.19-25. It says that atman is not born, nor does it die. It casts off worn-out bodies and enters into other new ones. No weapons can split it, nor fire burn it. No waters can wet it, nor wind dry it. The atman is invisible, unthinkable and unchanging.

According to the Advaita philosophy of Shankarāchārya a *jiva* is in bondage, goes through transmigration, and when free from *māyā*, it is identical to Brahman (Ultimate Reality). Shankarāchārya differentiates between *jiva* and atman, where one bound by *māyā* is called *jiva* and when that *jiva* becomes free of *māyā,* it is called atman. The bhakti Vedānta schools (founded by Rāmānujāchārya, Nimbārkāchārya, Madhavāchārya and others) consider *jiva,* atman or *jivātmā* to be atomic in size and innumerable,

The atman is sat-chit-ānanda

to pervade the physical body in which it resides and to be totally separate from and subservient to Brahman or God. Furthermore, it is important to note that the bhakti schools do not differentiate between *jiva* and atman as Shankarāchārya does. These schools understand the words *jiva,* atman and *jivātmā* to be synonymous, and by nature the *jiva* is pure and unbound by *māyā.* But when the *jiva* is bound by *māyā* (due to I-ness and My-ness) and goes through the cycle of births and deaths, they call it a *baddha* (bound) *jiva,* and when it is liberated, they call it a *mukta jiva.*

Hinduism believes that the *jivas* or atmans pervade the physical body it resides in *(sarva-gataha).*[13]

---

13. B.G. 2. 24.

5. KARMA

Karma means action or deed. Any physical, mental or emotional action is called karma. No living being can remain without performing actions for even a moment.[14] For every action there is a result or consequence. Hindus believe that karma is the universal law of cause and effect which governs life. It is a natural law of human life, just as gravity is a law of matter.

Hinduism teaches that a person's karma, past or present, is responsible for good or bad consequences in his or her life. It is also responsible for the disparities in life: rich and poor, high and low, intelligent or ordinary, good and bad. Hindus believe that nothing in our world is merely accidental or a chance happening.

The common wisdom, "As you sow, so shall you reap," succinctly sums up the Hindu law of karma. Good actions produce happiness and bad actions lead to suffering and misery in the present or future lives. Understanding the principle of karma can encourage a person to make moral and spiritual choices in his or her daily activities.

A prominent and early mention of the karma principle is found in the Brihadāranyaka Upanishad 3. 2.13, in which Sage Yājnavalkya tells Ārtabhāga, "Meritorious action leads to merit (punya), while evil action leads to further evil."

---

14. B.G. 3. 5-8.

Good deeds like charity confer merit (punya)

The Shvetāsvatara Upanishad 5.7 clearly states, "One who performs actions wanders in the cycle of transmigration according to his [good or bad] actions."

The law of karma is a moral principle that explains the circumstances and incidents in the present life to be the consequences of a person's deeds in the past or present lives. Nothing in one's life or in this world happens without a cause or reason. So a person's present or past governs his present and his present actions also shape his future. This means that every person is to some extent an architect of his own future.

There are two types of karmas that a person performs, namely, *nishkāma* and *sakāma*. *Nishkāma* karma means actions performed without any expectation of material gain,

65

ego and material desires, but solely done to perform one's duty (dharma) and please God. *Sakāma* karma means acts done for a specific material desire or purpose.

Karma is also categorized into three types:

i. *Kriyamāna* karma: The karma or action being performed every moment. The consequences or fruits of these karmas may be attained in this, the next or future lives.

ii. *Sanchita* karma: The vast accumulation of karma containing the sum total of all karmas done in one or many lives. The fruits of these karmas are being experienced or yet to be experienced.

iii. *Prārabdha* karma: The portion of one's *sanchita* karma that one is presently experiencing in this birth. For example, the attributes and conditions of one's physical body, mental capacities and circumstances are due to one's *prārabdha* karmas.

Hindus believe that God gives the fruits of one's good and bad karmas, that is, he is the karma *phala pradātā*. Karma or deed does not by itself produce or give results; it is only when God decides what to give as the fruits of one's karma that one actually experiences their positive or negative effects. It is worth noting that the karma principle is not applicable to animals because their actions are instinctual and they lack discrimination between right and wrong.

Bad deeds like violence, molestation and others incur sin (pāpa)

The principle of karma is not antithetical to the concept of human effort. As mentioned earlier, *kriyamāna* karma, that is doing karma every moment, is a part of the karma principle. Without daily action or deeds how can one hope to experience the result of present or past deeds! So karma does not negate the importance of human effort in any way.

Kim Knott mentions in her book[15] how Prof. Arvind Sharma deals with karma in his book *Hinduism for Our Times,* "To think fatalistically about karma is unhelpful when, in fact, as human beings we have the power at any moment to change our own behaviour, and thus its consequences for our future. Free will rather than fatalism characterizes the operation of karma." Karma is thus not fate, because

---

15. Knott, Kim. *Hinduism, A Very Short Introduction*. p. 39.

a person acts out of free will and is thus responsible for shaping his or her own destiny.

To dissolve or overcome the burden of karmas one has to perform good karmas, moral karmas and spiritual karmas with no desire for material gains *(nishkāma)*, and with the aim of pleasing God and the guru. Performing selfless karmas like service to mankind, praying, doing bhajan, reading or listening to shastras, performing bhakti of God, serving one's guru, etc. elevates one's soul. Through the performance of *nishkāma karmas,* one finally attains *moksha* by the grace of God or guru.

6. PUNARJANMA OR REBIRTH

Punarjanma or reincarnation or rebirth is the natural process of birth, death and rebirth. Hindus believe that the *jiva* or atman (soul) is intrinsically pure. However, because of the layers of I-ness and My-ness, the *jiva* goes through transmigration in the cycle of births and deaths. Death destroys the physical body, but not the *jiva*. The *jiva* is eternal. It takes on another body[16] with respect to its karmas. Every karma produces a result which must be experienced either in this or some future life. As long as the *jiva* is enveloped in ignorance, it remains attached to material desires and subject to the cycle of births and deaths. According to the

---

16. B.G. 2. 22.

Reincarnation is the natural process of birth, death and rebirth

Purāṇas, every *jiva* passes through 8,400,000 life forms. The four categories into which the *jiva* is born are: *udbhija* (born of seed, i.e. plants), *jarāyuja* (born of womb, i.e. mammals), *swedaja* (from sweat, i.e. bugs) and *andaja* (born of egg, i.e. birds and reptiles). Hindu texts such as the Purāṇas teach that the regression of a soul into animal bodies is due to its base karmas; similarly, the progression of the soul into human and divine bodies is due to its meritorious karmas. Birth in a human body is the highest and rarest of all births, because it provides the *jiva* an opportunity to achieve its main purpose: *mukti* or liberation.

Understanding *punarjanma* eliminates the fear of death. One realizes that one is not the body, but the immortal soul which takes on many bodies in its evolutionary sojourn through samsara. Reincarnation ends when one's karmas are resolved, God is realized and the fruit of *moksha* is attained.

What are the Reasons for Punarjanma?

There are several reasons why the *jiva* takes on different physical bodies:

i. To experience the fruits of one's karmas

This is the main reason for rebirth. A person's karmas influence his or her life and destiny. *Sāttvika* karmas i.e. good or righteous deeds, reward one with the pleasures of *swarga* (abode of the devas). *Rājas* karmas or pleasure-seeking material actions reward one with *mrutyuloka* (mortal realm or earth). And *tāmas* karmas, actions related to inertia, laziness and evil, condemn one to *pātāla-loka* (the lowest realm or the nether world). When the *jiva* exhausts its *sāttvika* karmas in *swarga*, it gets a human birth on earth.[17]

ii. To satisfy one's desires

When a person indulges in material pleasures, he or she subsequently develops a stronger desire to enjoy more of it (*vāsanās*). This unending craving to satisfy one's desires causes the *jiva* to assume new physical bodies.

17. B.G. 9.21.

iii. To complete one's unfinished sadhana

When an aspirant making spiritual efforts for liberation from *māyā* dies without attaining his goal, the *jiva* gets another human body to complete its sadhana.

iv. To fulfil a debt

When a *jiva* is indebted to another *jiva,* it gets a human birth to fulfil its debt and receive what is owed to it. The *jiva* comes in the form of a relative, friend or an enemy.

v. To undergo sufferings because of a great soul's curse

A person's grave error or sin may incur the wrath or displeasure of God or a rishi. This results in the *jiva* of that person getting another birth, not necessarily into a human body.

vi. To attain *moksha*

By the grace and compassion of God or a God-realized guru, a *jiva* gets a human body to purge itself of the layers of base instincts or moral and spiritual weaknesses.

When the *jiva* takes on another body, it is God who gives it an appropriate one in keeping with its karmas. When the *jiva* enters the new body it does so with its subtle (*sukshma*) and causal (*kārana*) bodies.

Sometimes the enlightened person (a *mukta*) takes birth by God's wish to carry out a special mission.

7. MURTI-PUJĀ

The worship of a sacred image of God, or his manifestations, or guru is known as *murti-pujā*. In Vedic times, the Indian rishis worshipped the forces of nature, namely, Varunadeva (sea-god), Indradeva (rain-god), Suryadeva (sun-god), Agnideva (fire-god), Vāyudeva (wind-god) and others. They revered and appeased these devas for their contributions in mankind's existence and happiness, by chanting various prayers in the form of mantras and by performing *yajnas*. Over time, they developed elaborate rituals of devotional worship for those devas and for the supreme God.

To facilitate their concentration on and worship of God, the rishis made *pratikas* (symbols) and *pratimās* (*murtis* or images) of clay, stone, metal and wood.[18] With consecration

---

18. In the Rig Veda (8.29) there is a beautiful description of the bodies, limbs and weapons of deities, and, according to it, Tvashtā is an artisan for the devas or deities as well as an architect. He is called *devashilpi* (1.20.6). It means that there must have been competent sculptors at that time. Later in the Vishnu Purāna (3.2.11) he is identified with Vishvakarmā – the famous sculptor, architect and engineer of the devas.

In the Kāthaka branch of the Krishna Yajur Veda (22.11) there is the mention of sage Devala who lived by preparing images. There is a reference to an image in the Sāma Veda (1.9.5) and the Atharva Veda refers to a temple (2.2.2.). The Sadvimsha Brāhmana text (5.10) not only mentions images but even the sculptor like Tvashtā. By the time of the Shrautasutras and Grihyasutras the worship of deities through images in temples were well established (Gautam Grihyasutra 3.7). Swami Harshananda. *A Concise Encyclopaedia of Hinduism,* Vol.2. Bangalore: Ramakrishna Matha, 2008, p.343.

| Stone | Wood | Metal | Sandalwood |

| Painting | Sand | Conceived by mind | Precious stone |

ceremonies, God was invoked (*prāna-pratishthā*) into a *murti*. Then the rishis regarded such a *murti* as God himself and not a statue. The *murti* became the focus and object of worship. The *murti* helps the aspirant to withdraw his mind and senses from material objects and concentrate on it. When the aspirant reaches the pinnacle of his sadhana, he realizes God, and he sees, speaks with and touches him.

The Shrimad Bhāgavata Purāna (11.27.12) describes eight types of God's *murtis*:

"Shaili dārumayi lauhi lepyā lekhyā cha saikati,
Manomayi manimayi pratimā ashtavidhā smrutā."

"A sacred image is made of one of eight materials: stone, wood, metal, sandalwood paste or clay (or other material

73

that can be moulded), sand, precious stones, conceived by mind and through painting or etching."

Professor Gavin Flood states, "Many Hindus believe in a transcendent God, beyond the universe, who is yet within all living beings and who can be approached in a variety of ways. The transcendent is mediated through icons in temples, through natural phenomena, or through living teachers and saints. Devotion [bhakti] to deities mediated through icons and holy persons provides refuge in times of crises and even final liberation [*moksha*] from action [karma] and the cycle of reincarnation [samsara]."[19]

In Bhakti Yoga the aspirant associates with the *murti* of God through devotion and love. He expresses his love through *sevā* and worship of God's *murti*. *Murti-pujā* has been practised for several centuries in India. Mandirs are built for darshan, worship, pilgrimage and service of God's *murti*. The worshippers of *murtis* and proponents of mandirs are followers of the Bhakti *sampradāya*, believing in God who always has a divine form *(sākāra)* even in his divine abode.

The Bhakti *sampradāyas* in Vaishnavism believe that the consecrated *murtis* of the supreme God and his manifestations in mandirs are not symbols but realities. Service of

---

19. Flood, Gavin. *An Introduction to Hinduism.* New Delhi: Cambridge University Press, Foundation Books, First South Asian Edition, 2004, pp. 10-11.

God means *seva* of his *murti*, which is an indispensable part of devotional practice for all Vaishnava devotees. Almost all Vaishnava, and many Shaiva, Shākta and Smārta shastras, called Āgamas, contain elaborate sections on rules, regulations and methods of *murti-pratishthā* and daily worship. One of the great teachers of

Devotion to God means adorning the image with clothes, jewellery and flowers

Shri Vaishnavism, Shri Pillai Lokācharya, in his work *Mumukshupadi* states, "The extreme limit of the easy accessibility that is mentioned here is the worshipped image. This form of the Lord [as *murti*] is our refuge. He holds the divine weapons in his hands. He keeps one of his hands in a posture asking us not to fear. He wears a crown. His face is smiling. His sacred body reveals that He is the protector and an object of enjoyment."[20]

For many Hindus who practise *murti-pujā* the devotional rituals provide joy and peace. Many also experience a sense of being near to God and understanding the futility of worldly pleasures.

---

20. Klostermaier K.K. *Hinduism, A Short History*, 2000, p.133.

8. GURU-SHISHYA PARAMPARĀ

The Guru and *Guru-shishya* (master-disciple) tradition is a unique feature of Hinduism. Since Upanishadic times the guru has played the role of imparting spiritual *(parā)* and mundane *(aparā)* knowledge *(vidyā)* to the disciple. The guru guides, inspires and also engages the disciple in the rigours of spiritual sadhana and worldly knowledge. Through spiritual disciplines he aids the disciple in realizing the Divine and in fulfilling the four *purushārthas* of human life.

For an aspirant bound by *māyā,* self-realization and God-realization are not possible without an adept guru. The guru must be *brahmanishtha* (God-realized) and *shrotriya* (one who knows and has realized the true meaning of the shastras) in order to liberate the aspirant. The *shishya* or disciple must be humble and totally obedient with unflinching faith in the guru.

The Hindu shastras and traditions speak glowingly of the guru as the form of God. The "God-realized" guru represents God, but he is not God. He purifies the disciple to make him eligible to experience the eternal bliss of God. So, by seeing, hearing, serving and thinking of the guru, one perceives and serves God. In this way, the guru is the bridge to and means of realizing God.

The guru *paramparā* or disciplic succession is central to the transmission of worldly and spiritual knowledge for most Hindus. Many Hindu traditions put great emphasis on two

Guru-shishya tradition: A guru blesses a disciple in his gurukula (tableau)

factors for transmission of knowledge: (1) its continuity or unbroken line of transmission and (2) importance of guru or teacher. Through the true spiritual guru, any given Hindu tradition is able to adhere to its core principles. The guru plays the role of a judge in interpreting those longstanding principles of Hinduism for new contexts and emerging conditions.

9. AHIMSA

Hindus believe in and practice the principle of ahimsa or nonviolence and non-killing. Ahimsa does not mean nonviolence in action alone, but also in thought and speech. Firstly, it is based on the Hindu beliefs that all living and non-living things are created by God and pervaded by him – *"Ishāvāsyam idam sarvam"* (i.e. "God pervades all things") – as stated in the Ishāvāsya Upanishad. Therefore everything is sacred.

Ahimsa teaches love and compassion for all living beings

Secondly, the majority of Hindus also believe there are separate and independent atmans in each living body, and God resides within all of them. From these two beliefs was born the principle of ahimsa and compassion for all living things.

Thirdly, the law of karma also deters one from violent and cruel actions or killing of any living being because of the adverse consequences to oneself.

Fourthly, the principle of *punarjanma* or rebirth operates in relation to good and bad karmas. A person who performs good karmas is rewarded with a happier and higher next life, whereas one who sins faces punishment, misery and degradation in this life or future lives.

Devout Hindus are generally vegetarian and abstain from killing or violence in any form. Ahimsa is one of the pillars of morality in Hinduism. Mahavir, Gandhiji and others were great apostles of ahimsa.

10. Four Purushārthas

All human beings have certain common desires to fulfil during their four stages of life. The ancient Indian seers recognized the four *purushārthas* or goals of human life to be basic and ideal. They are: (1) Dharma (righteousness, duty and moral order) to be performed, (2) *Artha* (wealth and prosperity) to be acquired, (3) *Kāma* (worldly desires) to be fulfilled and (4) *Moksha* (liberation) to be attained. In this way the ancient Hindus maintained a holistic perspective to human life and thus never neglected any aspect of it. The four goals or endeavours are the roadmap for a happy life on earth and beyond. The householders are guided to pursue all four goals, while the ascetics are ordained to focus on only two goals: dharma and *moksha*. Let us try to understand the goals briefly:

i. Dharma

Dharma is the foundation and first of the four principal human goals. It has its source in (1) Vedas (also known as Shruti), (2) tradition (also known as Smruti) and (3) customs of virtuous people. It is based on *ruta* (cosmic law) and *satya* (moral law). Dharma also refers to moral duties, obligations and conduct, namely, *vidhis* (dos) and *nishedhs* (don'ts). It includes *satya* (truthfulness), *saucha* (purity), *dayā* (compassion), ahimsa, *brahmacharya* (celibacy), *asteya* (non-stealing), *aparigraha* (non-possession), and *akrodha* (non-anger). Following dharma as prescribed by the Hindu shastras brings one *punya* (merit), success, fame and happiness. Furthermore, imbibing *ekāntika dharma,* which is superior to Varnāshrama Dharma because it consists of the virtues of dharma, *jnāna, vairagya* and bhakti, merits one with final liberation or *moksha*.

The Mahābhārata states, "If dharma is destroyed, it will destroy humanity and the world; If dharma is protected [i.e. practised], it will protect them."[21] It further declares, "Where there is dharma, there is victory."[22] In brief, dharma is the upholder, supporter and sustainer of society. It is the very essence of one's being.

ii. Artha

For progress and the fulfilment of dharma and *kāma,* wealth or *artha* is essential. Therefore the second life endeavour for the householder is the acquisition of wealth and material prosperity. The efforts and means to realize this goal must have a righteous and moral basis. They must be based on dharma or lawful means. Any wealth acquired through unethical ways

---

21. *"Dharma eva hato hanti, Dharmo rakshati rakshitah."* (Mahābhārata, Vana Parva, 313.128)

22. *"Yato dharmastato Krushno."* (Mahābhārata, Bhishma Parva, 43.60 and Shailya Parva, 62.32)

The four goals of human life: Dharma (righteousness), Artha (prosperity), Kāma (worldly desires) and Moksha (liberation)

does not give peace, happiness and prosperity. So, the basis of earning a living rests upon the foundation of dharma.

iii. Kāma

Fulfilment of biological, physical and material desires is the third goal. This mainly includes getting married and having a family. The householder is ordained by the shastras to legitimately fulfil his or her worldly desires in accordance to the canons of dharma.

Artha and *kāma* are important goals for the householder for the growth and progress of society.

iv. Moksha

Moksha means liberation from the web of *māyā*, freedom

from the cycle of births and deaths, and the eternal experience of divine happiness. This is the ultimate and final goal of human life. The atman within the human body is imperishable and eternal, unlike the body. But because of a person's ignorance, worldly desires and sinful karmas his or her atman goes through the cycle of births and deaths. The final objective of human life is to be liberated from mundane bondage and the cycle of births and deaths. This is achieved through refuge in God or a God-realized guru. Thereafter, through the guru's grace one becomes free from the bondage of *māyā*, and is blessed with self-realization and God-realization. Most of the Bhakti *sampradāyas* believe that when a devotee dies, his or her atman is blessed with a divine body, and it ascends to the supreme divine abode of God (*videha mukti*). Here, it forever resides, remaining blissfully absorbed in the darshan and *sevā* of Paramātmā. Some *sampradāyas* believe in being blessed with *mukti* while alive (*jivan-mukti*).

11. Varnāshrama Dharma

Hindu society had an organized social structure for the harmonious progress and development of individuals and society. It was called the *varnāshrama* system, which classified people into four classes (varnas) and stages (ashramas). Varna included the Brahmins, Kshatriyas, Vaishyas and Shudras;

Brahmins: Priests and teachers

Kshatriyas: Rulers and protectors

and ashrama meant the four stages of life, namely, Brahmacharya (student wedded to celibacy), Gruhastha (householder), Vānaprastha (retired life) and Sannyās (ascetic life).

The system, not practiced now, was originally based upon the personal qualities *(gunas)* and aptitudes for types of work (karmas) of individuals. It was not birth-based, i.e. caste system, as it later deviated to become.

The observance of *varnāshrama* dharma credited the individual with *punya* and thus the attainment of *swarga*.

SUMMARY

1. Two of the many fundamental beliefs that qualify a Hindu are that he or she believes in one Supreme Paramātmā who manifests in many forms, and the authority of the Vedas.

Vaishyas: Businessmen and farmers   Shudras: Weavers and labourers

2. The other important principles are *avatāravāda*, atman, karma, *punarjanma, murti-pujā, guru-shishya* tradition, ahimsa, four *purushārthas* and *varnāshrama dharma*.

3. *Avatāravāda* is the principle that God comes in human and other forms to liberate souls and eradicate evil.

4. Atman is the essence in all living things. It is *sat* (eternal), *chit* (consciousness) and *ānanda* (bliss) and separate from the body.

5. Karma means any physical, mental or emotional deed. It is not a self-operating system but is governed by God. God dispenses the fruits of one's karmas (as karma *phala pradāta*). Rebirth is a direct consequence of one's karmas.

6. *Punarjanma* means rebirth. The soul gets different life forms according to its karmas. Birth in a human body is

the greatest and most precious of all births.

7. *Murti-pujā* is a tradition based on the belief that God has a divine human and other forms. Since creation comprises shapes and forms, similarly, the creator too has a form. *Murti- pujā* enables the aspirant to focus his or her senses and mind on God.

8. The God-realized guru guides and liberates the *shishya* from the bondage of *māyā* and prepares him to lead a meaningful life in this world and the next. The *guru-shishya* tradition is an important facet of Hinduism.

9. Ahimsa means nonviolence in thought, speech and deed. Hindus believe that all things are created by God and pervaded by him. Therefore everything is believed to be sacred. Devout Hindus are generally vegetarian and abstain from killing in any form.

10. The four *purushārthas* are the four goals of human life. The rishis fully considered the needs of *brahmachāris* (celibate students), householders and ascetics by providing a roadmap of life. They guided householders to aspire for the four *purushārthas* or goals of human life, namely, dharma, *artha, kāma* and *moksha*, while encouraging the ascetics to focus on dharma and *moksha*.

11. *Varnāshrama* dharma means duties and responsibilities of Hindus in relation to their varnas (classes) and ashramas (stages of life).

Apollonius
Al-Biruni
Mark Twain

Romain Rolland
Ralph Waldo Emerson

Many travellers, pilgrims, scholars and statesmen have recognized and opined about the greatness of India's culture and Hinduism

4. IMPRESSIONS OF INDIA AND HINDUISM ABROAD

INTRODUCTION

To characterize Hinduism solely through India's present condition of comparative poverty, illiteracy, corruption and other ills, and to ignore its spiritual and cultural legacy of thousands of years, indicates an unbalanced or biased mind. Even today, the country's ancient heritage remains vibrant through many facets of its customs and traditions. It would be immature to characterize Hinduism in its entirety from a few of its cultural and social aberrations.

Such misconceptions and distortions about India fail to do justice to the Hindu traditions. One has to study and experience objectively to understand and grasp the truth and traditions of India's glorious culture and religion which have survived, flourished and contributed to world legacy for several millennia. India has survived one thousand years of foreign invasions and domination that had exploited, damaged and partly destroyed its culture and way of life. This is a testimony to its innate strength, purity and resilience.

India down the ages was blessed with some of the greatest minds and souls on earth. They had left no branch of human knowledge untouched. Their lofty contributions to the spiritual and temporal realms have been unparalleled. Many travellers, pilgrims, scholars and statesmen of different countries, religions, languages and cultures have hailed India as the 'Cradle of Civilization' and a 'Cultural Millionaire'. Studying their opinions and candid impressions offer penetrating insights and broad perspectives to the beauty and greatness of Hindu culture.

Sir John Malcolm (1769-1833 CE), the Governor of Bombay Presidency (which included much of Western and Central India) in the early 19th century, described the character of the Hindus, "The Hindoo inhabitants are a race of men, generally speaking, not more distinguished by their lofty stature, which rather exceeds that of Europeans, and their robust frame of body, than they are for some of the finest qualities of the mind; they are brave, generous, and humane, and their truth is as remarkable as their courage. I have known innumerable instances of its [honour] being carried to a pitch that would be considered in England, more fit for the page of a romance than a history: with regard to their fidelity, I think, as far as my knowledge extends, there are, generally speaking, no race of men more to be trusted."[1]

As the Bishop of Calcutta in the early 19th century Bishop Reginald Heber (1783-1826 CE) of England observed

---

1. Minutes of Evidence. London. 1813. pp.87 & 686.

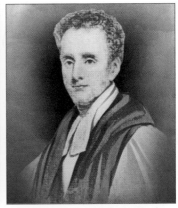

Sir John Malcolm (1769-1833 CE), Governor of Bombay Presidency

Reginald Heber (1783-1826 CE), Bishop of Calcutta

during his journey through India, "To say that the Hindus are deficient in any essential feature of a civilized people is an assertion which I can scarcely suppose to be made by any who have lived with them. They are decidedly by nature a mild, pleasing, intelligent race, sober and parsimonious, and, where an object is held out to them, most industrious and persevering. They are men of high and gallant courage, courteous, intelligent and most eager for knowledge and improvement, with a remarkable aptitude for the abstract sciences, geometry, astronomy, etc., and for imitative arts, painting and sculpture, dutiful towards their parents, affectionate to children, more easily affected by kindness and attention to their wants and feelings than almost any men I have met with. I have found in India a race of gentle

89

and temperate habits, with a natural talent and acuteness beyond the ordinary level of mankind."[2]

INFLUENCE ON GREECE, ROME AND EGYPT

Since ancient times India has been synonymous with trade, wealth, culture and Sanātana Dharma or Hinduism. It has been described as the fabled land that many men dreamed of.

Alexander the Great's foray into the fringe of Greater India in fourth century BCE left him contemplating the profound strength, character and spirituality of the people of India after his dialogue with King Porus and Dandāmis, a sannyasi. Megasthenes, the famous ancient Greek historian and ambassador to the court of Chandragupta Maurya, gives an interesting account of the incident. It begins with Onesikratês, one of Alexander's men, summoning Dandāmis, "King Alexander, who is the sovereign lord of all men, asks you to go to him, and if you comply, he will reward you with great and splendid gifts, but if you refuse will cut off your head."

Dandāmis replied fearlessly, "God, the supreme king, is

2. Sarda, Har Bilas. *Hindu Superiority: An Attempt to Determine the Position of the Hindu Race in the Scale of Nations.* Ajmer: Rajputana Printing Works, 1906, pp.42-43. Har Bilas Sarda (B.A., F.R.S.L.) was a Member of the Royal Asiatic Society of Great Britain and Ireland; Fellow of the Royal Statistical Society of London; and Member of the Statistical Association of Boston, United States.

never the author of insolent wrong, but is the creator of light, of peace, of life, of water, of the body of man, and of souls. He alone is the God of my homage, who abhors slaughter and instigates no wars." Further, Dandāmis told Onesikratês, "But Alexander is not God, since he must taste of death, and how can such as he be the

A scene from a drama presentation of King Alexander and Sage Dandāmis' encounter

world's master, who has not yet reached the further shore of the River Tiberoboas.

"Know this, however, that what Alexander offers me, and the gifts he promises, are all things to me utterly useless. I lie upon the forest leaves, and, having nothing which requires guarding, close my eyes in tranquil slumber. The earth supplies me with everything.

"Should Alexander cut off my head, he cannot also destroy my soul. When we depart hence to his [God's] presence, an account of our life, for the groans of the oppressed become the punishments of the oppressors.

"Let Alexander, then, terrify with these threats those who wish for gold and for wealth, since the Bragmanes [Brahmins]

91

neither love gold nor fear death. Go, then, tell Alexander this: 'Dandāmis has no need of aught that is yours, and therefore will not go to you, but if you want anything from Dandāmis come you to him.'"[3]

On hearing this, Alexander felt a strong desire to see Dandāmis because he was the only antagonist in whom he, the conqueror of many nations, had met his match.

Merchants from Egypt travelled to India to avail themselves of its wealth and knowledge. Recent archaeological excavations have revealed a site of a Roman colony at Arikamedu in south India. From this site, there is evidence that the Romans imported luxury goods from India.

William Enfield, a British theologian, writes, "We find that it [India] was visited, for the purpose of acquiring knowledge, by Pythagoras, Anaxarchus, Pyrrho, and others, who afterwards became eminent philosophers in Greece. Some of the doctrines of the Greeks concerning nature are said to have been derived from the Indians."[4]

Professor A.A. Macdonell (1854-1930 CE), Oxford Boden professor of Sanskrit of Corpus Christi College, writes, "According to Greek tradition, Thales, Empedocles, Anaxagoras, Democritus, and others undertook journeys to Oriental countries in order to study philosophy. The influence of In-

---

3. Megasthenes and Arrian. *Ancient India*. Translated by J.W. McCrindle. London: Trübner & Co, 1877, pp.124-126.

4. Dr Enfield. *History of Philosophy*, Vol.1. p. 65.

Empedocles (c. 490-430 BCE),
Greek philosopher

Anaxagoras (c. 500-428 BCE),
Greek philosopher

dian philosophy on Christian Gnosticism in the second and third centuries [CE] seems at any rate undoubted. The Gnostic doctrine of the opposition between the soul and matter, of the personal existence of intellect, will, and so forth, the identification of soul and light, are derived from the Sankhya system. Again Bardesanes, a Gnostic of the Syrian school, who obtained information about India from Indian philosophers, assumed the existence of a subtle ethereal body which is identical to the *linga sharir* (subtle body) of the Sankhya System."[5]

Friedrich von Schlegel (1772-1829 CE), a German poet, critic and scholar, says, "The doctrine of the transmigration of souls was indigenous to India and was brought into

---

5. Macdonell, A.A. *A History of Sanskrit Literature*. New York: D. Appleton and Company, 1900, pp.422 & 423.

Friedrich von Schlegel,
German poet, critic and scholar

Greece by Pythagoras."[6]

Indians had travelled to several European countries and after settling there they preserved their culture and religion. Mr E. Pococke, author of *India in Greece,* states, "Now, the whole of this state of society (Greece), civil and military, must strike every one as being eminently Asiatic; much of it specifically Indian. Such it undoubtedly is; and I shall demonstrate that these evidences were but the attendant tokens of an Indian colonisation, with its corresponding religion and language. I shall exhibit dynasties disappearing from western India, to appear again in Greece: clans, whose martial fame is still recorded in the faithful chronicles of northwestern India, as the gallant bands who fought upon the plains of Troy; and, in fact, the whole of Greece, from the era of the supposed god-ships of Poseidon and Zeus, down to the close of the Trojan war, as being Indian in language, sentiment, and religion, and in the arts of peace and war."[7] Mr Pococke

---

6. Sarda, Har Bilas. *Hindu Superiority.* p.280; *History of Literature.* p.109.

7. Pococke, E. *India in Greece.* London: John J. Griffin And Co., 1852, p.12.

further confirms, "The early civilization then – the early arts – the indubitably early literature of India, are equally the civilization, the arts and the literature of Egypt and of Greece – for geographical evidences, conjoined to historical fact, and religious practices, now prove beyond all dispute,

Pythagoras (c. 570-495 BCE), Greek philosopher and mathematician

that the two latter countries are the colonies of the former."[8]

APOLLONIUS OF TURKEY

Apollonius of Tyana was a physician who lived in Turkey in 100 CE. Much of what we know about Apollonius today comes from a biography written by Philostratus, a prominent Greek intellectual of the 2nd and 3rd century.[9]

Philostratus notes that Apollonius was a follower of Pythagoras (c. 570-495 BCE), a Greek philosopher and mathematician, who lived six centuries earlier. Apollonius

8. Ibid. p.74.
9. Philostratus, the Athenian (2nd/3rd century). Translated by Phillimore, John Swinnerton., In *Honour of Apollonius of Tyana*, Vol.1. Oxford: Clarendon Press, 1912, pp.107-110.

believed that many of Pythagoras' teachings like reincarnation, vegetarianism, observing silence as a spiritual discipline and others, were all a part of Hindu tradition. Apollonius travelled to India, and with the help of a local king he was introduced to a yogi named Iarchas. The yogi welcomed him by name, and told him his parents' names and mentioned a few facts and incidents about Apollonius's life. Apollonius was surprised and asked the yogi how he knew so much about him. Iarchas replied, "By knowing ourselves."

In the months that Apollonius stayed Iarchas taught him disciplines and rituals through intensive yogic training, the Vedic method of performing puja and other Hindu techniques. Apollonius learned to use mantras and how to empower *yantras* (sacred diagrams). For centuries after his death, the *yantras* empowered by Apollonius were known throughout the Western world for their miraculous properties.

Apollonius travelled throughout the Roman Empire, from Spain, to Africa and to India. Noting his experiences in India he wrote, "I have seen men dwelling on the earth but not of the earth. I saw them well defended without fortifications. I saw they owned nothing, yet possessed all things."

Apollonius travelled to Egypt and up the Nile, he met the

desert ascetics of Ethiopia whose spiritual beliefs and practices were similar to the ascetics he had met and stayed with in India. On further enquiry he found evidence that the forefathers of these Ethiopians had emigrated from India. This is confirmed by an account on Egypt's history in

Apollonius of Tyana,
physician who lived in Turkey, 100 CE

Greek by Manetho, an Egyptian priest. He wrote that the immigrants from northern India settled in Ethiopia around 1400 BCE.

Apollonius travelled widely in the Western world and in Egypt and Persia most of his life. He noted that nowhere did he find and experience the lofty wisdom and knowledge as he had found in India. He claimed that many of the mystic schools of the West had their origin in India. He wrote a four-volume book about the Hindu spiritual wisdom, which unfortunately is lost to us. Apollonius was one of the most revered and famous spiritual teachers in the Western world during the initial several centuries of the Common Era.

INDIAN DEVAS AND DEVIS IN TURKEY, PERSIA AND ROME

Another fact that shows the West had an Indian connection was the worship of goddess Magna Mater[10] or 'Great Mother' in Turkey since at least 800 BCE. In 204 BCE a Roman delegation brought an image of Magna Mater from Phrygia in Asia Minor to Rome to enable them to win their war against Carthage. The goddess remained the patron deity of Rome till Rome's conversion to Christianity. The Magna Mater was discovered to be the Indian goddess Durgā. Even today, 300 ft. up the north face of Mount Sipylus in Turkey one can find an ancient 30 ft. high image of the goddess carved into solid rock.

Magna Mater, her Latin name, means "Great Mother", which is similar to Durgā's title, Mahā Devi (Great Goddess) or Shri Mātā (Respected Mother), in India. In ancient Turkey Magna Mater was known as Truquas, whom scholars believe is related to her Indian name, Durgā.

Other Hindu devas were worshipped in Turkey in ancient times. Renowned Indian archaeologist B.B. Lal explains that in 1500 BCE, the Mitanni people of Turkey worshipped and appeased Indra (rain-god), Mitra (sun-god), Varuna (sea-god) and the Ashwinis (physicians of the de-

---

10. Johnsen, Linda. *The Complete Idiot's Guide to Hinduism*. Indianapolis, USA: Alpha books, 2002, pp.37-38.

vas). He writes, "The Bog-haz Kuei inscription, dating back to the fourteenth century BC, refers to Indra, Mitra, Nāsatya and Varuna as witnesses to a treaty between the Mitanni King Matiwaza and the Hittite King Suppiluliuma.

Murti of Varuna Deva (Sea-god)

"The renowned scholar, T. Burrow (1955) came to the conclusion: 'The Aryans appear in Mitanni from 1500 BC as the ruling dynasty.' Around 1500 BC there was no other country in the entire world except India where the above mentioned gods were worshipped."[11] Thus Mitra was worshipped in India in 4000 BCE and beyond, and was worshipped as Mithras by the Persians, and was also the patron deity of the Roman army.

CHINESE PILGRIMS TO INDIA AND INDIA'S INFLUENCE ON SOUTHEAST ASIA

Two of the most important accounts about ancient India are by two Chinese Buddhist pilgrims. Fa-xian (337- c.422 CE), also known as Fa-hsien or Fa-hien, came to India around

11. Lal, B.B. *The Homeland of the Aryans*. New Delhi: Aryan Books International, 2005, p.84.

Hsüan-tsang, Chinese Buddhist pilgrim

400 CE and Xuanzang (602-664 CE), also known as Hsüan-tsang, came to North India in 629 CE. At the time of his visit, Fa-xian was impressed by the peace, prosperity and noble culture of the Hindus. At that time China was torn by internal wars. Fa-xian saw that the leaders in India fostered commerce, culture and religion rather than destroying large numbers of their population. He wrote that one could travel in India without fear of crime, and that the country was safe, stable and religious.

Xuanzang studied Sanskrit, logic, grammar and Buddhist philosophy at the Nālandā University in Magadha (Bihar), where about 3,000 Buddhist monks and 150 professors resided. Students from all parts of the world came there to study. The academic curriculum also included the Vedas, Vedic mathematics, astronomy, astrology, medical science and literature.

Hsüan-tsang wrote, "Though Indians are of a light temperament, they are distinguished by the straightforwardness and honesty of their character. With regard to riches, they never take anything unjustly; with regard to justice, they make even excessive concessions. Straightforwardness is the distinguishing feature of their administration."[12]

Takakusu Junjiro (1866-1945 BCE), a Japanese scholar, writes in his book *I-Tsing* about the famous Chinese traveller's (I-Tsing, 635-713 CE) visit to India in 673 BCE. From his records one finds about India's outreach to several neighbouring eastern countries. "The whole coast of farther India from Suvarnabhumi (Indonesia) or Burma to China, and also of the islands of the Malay Archipelago, was studded with prosperous Indian colonies and naval stations, which ocean-liners regularly plying in the eastern waters between India and China constantly used as convenient halting places. I-Tsing refers to more than ten such colonies where Indian manners, customs, and religious practices prevailed together with Sanskrit learning. These were Sri-Bhoja (Pelambang) in Sumatra, Kalinga in Java, Mahasin in Borneo (Barhinadwipa), and the islands of Bali, Bhojapara, etc., which had all Indian names, and afforded to Chinese pilgrims to India a good preparatory training."[13]

---

12. Müller, F.Max. *India, What Can It Teach Us?* New Delhi: Penguin Books, 2000, p.51.

13. Mookerji, Radhakumud. *A History of Indian Shipping and Maritime Activity from the Earliest Times.* London and New York: Longmans, Green and Co., 1912, p. 171.

AL BIRUNI IN INDIA

Born in 973 CE, Al Biruni (973-1048 CE) lived in Khwarizm, today's Khiva in Uzbekistan. He was a brilliant Arab astrologer and scholar who wrote books on chemistry, mathematics, mineral science, optics, mechanics and the dating systems and calendars of many

Al Biruni, Arab astrologer and scholar

nations. Khwarizm was looted by the Muslim raider Abu-Said Mahmud (Mahmud Ghazni) in 1017 CE. Al Biruni was taken to India by Mahmud where the former lived for 13 years. During his stay Al Biruni studied Sanskrit and learnt science and spirituality from the Hindu pundits. He wrote a voluminous study of Hindu culture and spirituality called *Kitabul Hind (Alberuni's India)*. He has noted the Hindu view of God in his book saying that the Hindus believed in one God and that he is beyond the perception of mind and senses. He further noted that to attain him and experience his bliss single-minded meditation on him was necessary.

OTHER SCHOLARS AND THINKERS

In the 18th century, many British, French, American

and other intellectuals were especially impressed by Hinduism and India's people and culture.

Sir John R. Seeley (1834-1895 CE), Professor of Modern History in Cambridge University, writes about India, "Perhaps no race has shown a greater aptitude for civilization. Its customs grew

Mark Twain, American author

into laws, and were consolidated in codes. It imagined the division of labour. It created poetry and philosophy and the beginnings of science. We [British] are not cleverer than the Hindu; our minds are not richer or larger than his. We cannot astonish him, as we astonish the barbarians, by putting before him ideas that he never dreamed of. He can match from his poetry our sublimest thoughts; even our science perhaps has few conceptions that are altogether novel to him."[14]

Mark Twain (1835-1910 CE), an American author and humourist, praises India, "This is indeed India; the land of dreams and romance; of fabulous wealth, cradle of the human race, birthplace of human speech, mother of history,

---

14. Seeley, Sir John R. *The Expansion of England*. London: Macmillan and Co. Ltd., 1914, pp.279 & 283.

Prof. Will Durant, American historian   Romain Rolland, French savant

grandmother of legend, great-grandmother of tradition. The one land that all men desire to see, and having seen once, by even a glimpse, would not give that glimpse for the shows of all the rest of the globe combined. There is only one India! It is the only country that has a monopoly of grand and imposing specialties. In religion all other countries are paupers; India is the only millionaire."[15]

Prof. Will Durant (1885-1981 CE), an American author and historian, writes that India is the mother of our spiritual and mundane realms, "That India was the motherland of our race, and Sanskrit the mother of Europe's languages; that she was the mother of our philosophy, mother, through

15. Twain, Mark. *Following the Equator, A Journey Around the World.* Hartford: American Publishing Co., New York: Doubleday & McClure Co., 1897, pp. 347, 348, 397.

the Arabs, of much of our mathematics, mother, through Buddha, of the ideals embodied in Christianity, mother, through the village community, of self-government and democracy. Mother India is in many ways the Mother of us all."[16]

Romain Rolland (1866-1944 CE), a French author, writes highly of India, "If there is one place on the face of the earth where all the dreams of living men have found a home from the very earliest days when man began the dream of existence, it is India."[17]

SOCIAL, SCIENTIFIC AND SPIRITUAL CONTRIBUTIONS OF INDIA

In the domains of social, scientific and spiritual knowledge, ancient India had made remarkable strides. Its rishis or great spiritual masters, through their powers of self-realization and God-realization, had explored various realms of human knowledge. Some testimonies of Western scholars who generously appreciated the genius of Indians are as follows.

1. Currency, Government and Social System

The Hindus, it seems, were the first to have coined money, and as pointed out by Princep, "The Hindus were at least 800

---

16. Durant, Will. *The Case for India*. New York: Simon and Schuster, 1930, p.4.
17. Rolland, Romain. *Prophets of the New India*. Translated by E.F. Malcolm Smith. London: Cassell and Company Ltd., 1930, p.4.

years before Christ in possession of elaborate schemes of exchange. They had developed an excellent system of government suited to the times and the laws propounded by them were foundations of the Egyptian, Persian, Grecian and the Roman code of law."[18]

Writers and thinkers like Coleman, Dr Robertson, Prof. Wilson and others admired the laws and civic system set up by the Indians by saying that the social organization of the ancient Hindus showed a highly advanced stage of civilization and culture.

Louis Jacolliot (1837-1890 CE), a French author and lecturer, in his book *The Bible in India* said, "Manou [Manu] inspired Egyptian, Hebrew, Greek, and Roman legislation, and his spirit still permeates the whole economy of our European laws."[19]

2. Medicine and Surgery

With reference to the pioneering work of medicine in India, experts believe that Ayurveda is the oldest system of medicine in the world. They explain that if Ayurveda had its source from Greek medicine, it would have at least some

---

18. Chand Narang, Gokul, *Real Hinduism*. New Delhi: New Book Society of India, 1999, p.29.

19. *The Bible in India: Hindoo Origin of Hebrew and Christian Revelation*. Translated from "La Bible Dans L'Inde" by Louis Jacolliot. New York: Carleton Publisher; London: J.C. Hotten, 1883, p. xii.

words that are similar to the Greek words. Prof. Dominik Wujastyk, a scholar on Ayurveda, in his article 'The Science of Medicine', states, "It [is] even more striking that not one Greek loanword for a medical term appears in Sanskrit medical literature."[20] This fact helps validate the antiquity and originality of Ayurveda.

Oliver Russell, 2nd Baron Ampthill (1869-1935 CE), Governor of Madras, said in 1905, "Now we are beginning to find out that the Hindu Shastras also contain a Sanitary Code no less correct in principal, and that the great law-giver, Manu, was one of the greatest sanitary reformers the world has ever seen. They can lay claim to have been acquainted with the main principles of curative and preventive medicine at a time when Europe was still immersed in ignorant savagery. I am not sure whether it is generally known that the science of medicine originated in India, but this is the case, and the science was first exported from India to Arabia and thence to Europe. Down to the close of the seventeenth century, European physicians learnt the science from the works of Arabic doctors; while the Arabic doctors many centuries before had obtained their knowledge from the works of great Indian physicians such as Dhanwantari, Charaka and Susruta."[21]

---

20. The Blackwell Companion to Hinduism, edited by Gavin Flood. Oxford: Blackwell Publishing, 2005, p.395.

21. Sarda, Har Bilas. *Hindu Superiority*. Ajmer: Rajputana Printing Works, 1906, pp.301 & 307.

According to Prof. H.H. Wilson (1796-1860 CE), "The ancient Hindus attained as thorough a proficiency in medicine and surgery as any people whose acquisitions are recorded."[22]

Sir William Hunter (1840-1900 CE), a British historian and Vice-President of the Asiatic Society, described the expanse and depth that Indian medicine had acquired, "Indian medicine dealt with the whole area of the science. It described the structure of the body, its organs, ligaments, muscles, vessels and tissues. The *Materia Medica* of the Hindus embraces a vast collection of drugs belonging to the mineral, vegetable and animal kingdoms, many of which have now been adopted by European physicians. Their pharmacy contained ingenious processes of preparation, with elaborate directions for the administration and classification of medicines. Much attention was devoted to hygiene, to the regimen of the body, and to diet."[23]

With reference to surgery, Albrecht Friedrich Weber (1825-1901 CE), a German Indologist and historian, notes, "In surgery, too, the Indians seem to have attained a special proficiency, and in this department European surgeons might perhaps even at the present day still learn something from them, as indeed they have already borrowed from

---

22. Ibid. p.302.

23. Hunter, W.W. *The Imperial Gazetteer of India,* Vol. VI, 2nd edn. London: Trübner & Co., 1886, p.107.

them the operation of rhinoplasty [making artificial noses and ears]."[24]

In *Ancient and Mediaeval India* Mrs. Manning states, "The surgical instruments of the Hindus were sufficiently sharp, indeed, as to be capable of dividing a hair longitudinally."[25]

Sir William Hunter revealed, "The surgery of the ancient Indian physicians appears to have been bold and skilful. They conducted amputations; practised lithotomy; performed operations in the abdomen and uterus; cured hernia, fistula, piles; set broken bones and dislocations; and were dexterous in the extraction of foreign substances from the body. A special branch of surgery was devoted to rhinoplasty, or operations for improving deformed ears and noses, and forming new ones; a useful operation which European surgeons have borrowed."[26]

Furthermore, Sir William Hunter stated, "The Hindu medicine is an independent development. Arab medicine was founded on the translations of Sanskrit treatises made by command of the Khalif of Baghdad (950-960 AD). European medicine down to the 17th century was based upon

---

24. Weber, Albrecht. *The History of Indian Literature*. Translated from the second German edition by John Mann and Theodor Zachariae. London: Kegan Paul, Trench, Trübner & Co. Ltd., 1878, pp.269-270.

25. Mrs. Manning. *Ancient and Mediaeval India*, Vol. II. London: Wm. H. Allen & Co., p.346; Sarda, Har Bilas. *Hindu Superiority*. p.303.

26. Hunter, W.W. *The Imperial Gazetteer of India*, Vol.V1, 2nd edn. London: Trübner & Co., 1886, pp.107-108.

the Arabic, and the name of the Indian physician, Charaka, repeatedly occurs in Latin translations of *Avicenna* (Abu Sina), *Rhazes* (Abu Rasi) and *Serapion (*Abu Sirabi).[27]

India was also the first country to institute hospitals, and for centuries her doctors are believed to be the only ones in the world who maintained them. In the 5th century, the Chinese Buddhist pilgrim, Fa-xian, described a hospital he visited in Pātaliputra, "Hither come all poor and helpless patients suffering from all kinds of infirmities. They are well taken care of, and a doctor attends them: food and medicine being supplied according to their wants. Thus they are made quite comfortable, and when they are well, they may go away."[28] In contrast, the earliest hospital in Europe, as pointed out by Vincent Smith, was opened in the tenth century.

3. Mathematics

According to Mrs. Manning, "To whatever cyclopaedia, journal or essay we refer, we uniformly find our numerals traced to India and the Arabs recognised as the medium through which they were introduced into Europe."[29]

The mastery of the Hindus in mathematics has also been generally recognized and appreciated. The great German

---

27. Sarda, Har Bilas. *Hindu Superiority.* p.307.

28. Smith, Vincent A. *The Early History of India,* 3rd edn. New Delhi: Atlantic Publishers and Distributors, 1999, p. 296.

29. Sarda, Har Bilas. *Hindu Superiority.* p.320.

*Mountstuart Elphinstone,
Scottish statesman and historian*

*Monier Williams, Boden Professor of
Sanskrit, Oxford University*

philosopher, Friedrich von Schlegel, says, "The decimal cyphers, the honour of which, next to letters the most important of human discoveries, has, with the common consent of historical authorities, been ascribed to the Hindus."[30]

Mr Mountstuart Elphinstone (1779-1859 CE) a Scottish statesman and historian, and Governor of Bombay, pointed out, "Their [Hindus] geometrical skill is shown, among other forms, by their demonstrations of various properties of triangles, and was unknown in Europe till published by Clavins."[31] Sir Monier Williams (1819-1899 CE), the great Sanskrit lexicographer of England, averred, "Whatever conclusions we may arrive at as the original source of the first astronomical

---

30. Ibid. pp.319-320; Schlegel. *History of Literature*, p.123.

31. Elphinstone, Mountstuart. *The History of India*, Vol.1. Second Edition. London: John Murray, 1843, pp.250-251.

*Henry Thomas Colebrooke,
British Orientalist and Director of the
Royal Asiatic Society*

ideas current in the world, it is probable that to the Hindus is due the invention of algebra and its application to astronomy and geometry."[32]

Mr Henry Thomas Colebrooke (1765-1837 CE), a British Orientalist and Director of the Royal Asiatic Society, wrote, "Their application of algebra to astronomical investigations and geometrical demonstrations is also an invention of their own; and their manner of conducting it is even now entitled to admiration."[33]

The Europeans are often erroneously credited with the discovery of differential calculus, however, many of its principles have been traced centuries earlier to the works of Bhāskarāchārya II (1114-1183 CE), who was one of the greatest Indian mathematicians.

4. Astronomy

Mr Elphinstone said, "Proofs of very extraordinary

32. Williams, Monier. *Indian Wisdom,* Third Edition. London: Wm.H. Allen & Co., 1876, p.184.

33. Sarda, Har Bilas. *Hindu Superiority*. p.329.

proficiency in their astronomical writings are found."[34] As expressed by Mr Weber, "Astronomy was practiced in India as early as 2780 BCE."[35]

The Hindus had discovered the motion of the earth on its axis in 500 BCE. They had calculated the length of the year to be 365 days, 5 hours, 50 minutes, 35 seconds, long before French Astronomer Callie calculated it to be 365 days, 5 hours, 48 minutes, 49 seconds. Prof. H.H. Wilson (1796-1860 CE) says, "The originality of Hindu astronomy is at once established, but it is also proved by intrinsic evidence, and although there are some remarkable coincidences between the Hindu and other systems, their methods are their own."[36]

Mr H.T. Colebrooke wrote, "Aryabhatta affirmed the diurnal revolution of the earth on its axis. He possessed the true theory of the causes of solar and lunar eclipses, and disregarded the imaginary dark planets of mythologists and astrologers, affirming the moon and primary planets {and even the stars} to be essentially dark and only illumined by the sun."[37]

5. Architecture

From excavations in Mohenjo-daro, Harappa, Lothal,

---

34. Ibid p.333.

35. Ibid. p.333.

36. Ibid. p.338-339; Mill. *History of India,* Vol. II. p. 107.

37. Colebrooke, H.T. *Miscellaneous Essays*, Vol.13. London: Trübner & Co, 1873, p.421.

An illustration of the town of Harappa

Dholavira and other places, we find that the layout, houses and streets of these towns of the Indus Valley civilization show that its people had advanced knowledge about architectural and town planning. The streets of Harappa had a grid pattern, its houses had good sanitary arrangements. While small houses had two rooms and large ones up to twenty-five rooms, and their big granaries had a striking feature. In Mohenjo-daro 'The Great Bath' was one of the chief attractions. "A far higher degree of development was attained by architecture, of which some most admirable monuments still remain."[38] Mr Thornton stated, "The ancient Indians erected buildings, the solidity of which has not been overcome by the revolution of thousands of years."[39]

Describing the temple of Rameshwaram, Lord Valentia said, "The whole building presents a magnificent

---

38. Weber, Albrecht. *The History of Indian Literature*. Translated from the second German Edition by John Mann and Theodor Zachariae. London: Kegan Paul, Trench, Trübner & Co. Ltd, 1878, p.274.

39. Sardar, Har Bilas. *Hindu Superiority*. p.390.

appearance, which we might in vain seek adequate language to describe."[40]

6. Sanskrit and Vedic Literature

Prof. Max Müller (1823-1900 CE), an Oxford Sanskrit scholar, stated, "That literature [ancient literature of India] opens to us a chapter in what has been called the Education of the Human Race, to which we can find no parallel anywhere else."[41] When the Yajur Veda was presented to the French philosopher, Voltaire, he exclaimed that, "It was the most precious gift for which the West had been ever indebted to the East."[42] According to Guigault, "The Rig Veda is the most sublime conception of the great highways of humanity."[43]

Sir Monier Williams writing about Panini, the great Indian Sanskrit grammarian, stated, "No other country can produce any grammatical system at all comparable to it, either for originality of plan or analytical subtlety. The Sutras of Pānini are indeed a perfect miracle of condensation."[44]

---

40. Heeren, A.H.L. *Historical Researches into the Politics, Intercourse, and Trade of the Principal Nations of Antiquity.* London: Henry G. Bohn, 1866, p.92; Valentia. *Travels,* Vol. I. p.340.

41. Müller, F. Max. *India, What Can It Teach Us?* New Delhi: Penguin Books, 2000, p.81.

42. Sardar, Har Bilas. *Hindu Superiority.* p.220; *Wilson's Essays,* Vol.III, p.304.

43. Ibid. p.220.

44. Williams, Monier. *Indian Wisdom.* 3rd ed. London: Wm. H. Allen & Co., 1876, pp.172 & 174.

Speaking about the Rāmāyana, Ralph Griffith (1826-1906 CE), a translator of the Vedas, says, "Nowhere else are poetry and morality so charmingly united, each elevating the other as in this really holy poem."[45]

Speaking of the epic poems of Vālmiki and Vyāsa, namely, the Rāmāyana and the Mahābhārata, A. Barth, a French scholar, says, "It is not in size alone that the sacred epics of Vālmiki and Vyāsa excel. They enchant by the wondrous story they tell of ancient Aryan life, faith and valour. Matchless vivacity, unsurpassably tender and touching episodes, and a perfect storehouse of national antiquities, literature and ethics."[46]

"In the composition of tales and fables," says Elphinstone, "they [Hindus] appear to have been the instructors of the rest of mankind."[47] They were translated into Arabic, Persian, Greek, Spanish, Hebrew, Chinese, etc. hundreds of years ago.

7. Vedas, Upanishads and Bhagavad Gītā

With reference to Indian philosophy, Prof. Max Müller observed, "The Hindus were a nation of philosophers, such as could nowhere have existed except in India."[48] Schlegel

---

45. Sarda, Har Bilas. *Hindu Superiority*. pp.234-235.

46. Ibid. p.239.

47. Ibid. p.263.

48. Bunsen, Christian Charles, *Outlines of the Philosophy of Universal History*, Vol.1. London: Longman, Brown, Green and Longmans, 1845, p.132.

speaks of the noble, clear and grand aspects of Indian thought, "Even the loftiest philosophy of the Europeans, the idealism of reason, as is set forth by Greek philosophers, appears in comparison with the abundant light and vigour of Oriental idealism like a feeble Promethean spark in the full flood of heavenly glory of the noonday sun – faltering and feeble and ever-ready to be extinguished."[49]

Dr Alexander Duff (1806-1878 CE), a Christian missionary, spoke of the Hindu philosophy, "Hindu philosophy was so comprehensive that counterparts of all systems of European philosophy were to be found in it."[50] Prof. Goldstücker (1821-1872 CE), a German Sanskrit scholar, finds in the Upanishads "the germs of all the philosophies."[51] Speaking of the practical nature of Hindu philosophy, Count Bjornstjerna (1779-1847 CE), a Swedish diplomat and writer, says, "The Hindus were far in advance of the philosophers of Greece and Rome."[52] Mr. Colebrooke, the eminent antiquarian, thought, "The Hindus were the teachers and not the learners."[53] Sir Monier Williams thought Pythagoras and Plato both believed in the doctrine of "transmigration of souls" and thought they were indebted for it to Hindu writ-

49. Ibid. p.276.
50. Ibid. p.277.
51. Ibid. p.277
52. Ibid. p.279.
53. Ibid. p.279

*Arthur Schopenhauer, (1788-1860 CE),
German philosopher*

ers. Prof. Macdonell gleaned how the Sānkhya system of Hindu philosophy influenced Christian Gnosticism in the second and third centuries. Even in modern times, the serene and magnificent philosophy of the Upanishads has influenced some of the greatest men of the West.

Arthur Schopenhauer (1788-1860 CE), the great 19th century German philosopher and writer, whom Max Müller described as a rigorous logician, said, "From every sentence [of the Upanishads] deep, original, and sublime thoughts arise, and the whole is pervaded by a high and holy and earnest spirit. And oh, how thoroughly is the mind here washed clean of all early engrafted Jewish superstitions, and of all philosophy that cringes before those superstitions! In the whole world there is no study, except that of the originals, so beneficial and so elevating as that of the Oupnekhat [Upanishads]. It has been the solace of my life, it will be the solace of my death![54] Writing on this,

---

54. *The Sacred Books of the East.* Edited by F. Max Müller, translated by various Oriental Scholars. Oxford: Clarendon Press, 1879, p.1xi.

Max Müller says, "Schopenhauer was the last man to write at random, or to allow himself to go into ecstasies over so-called mystic and inarticulate thought. And I am neither afraid nor ashamed to say that I share his enthusiasm for the Vedanta [Upanishads], and feel indebted to it for much

Max Müller, (1823-1900 CE), Western scholar

that has been helpful to me in my passage through life."[55] Furthermore Max Müller adds, "The Upanishads, the remote sources of Indian philosophy, and especially of the Vedanta philosophy, a system in which human speculation seems to me to have reached its very acme."[56]

When Ralph Waldo Emerson (1803-1882 CE), an American essayist, philosopher and poet, read a translation of the Bhagavad Gita he praised, "I owed a magnificent day to the Bhagavad Gita. It was the first of books; it was as if an empire spake to us, nothing small or unworthy, but large, serene, consistent, the voice of an old intelligence which in another age and climate had pondered and thus

55. Müller, F.M. *The Six Systems of Indian Philosophy.* New York: Longmans, Green, and Co. London and Bombay, 1899, p.253.

56. Ibid. p.v.

Ralph Waldo Emerson (1803-1882 CE),
American essayist, philosopher
and poet

Henry David Thoreau (1817-1862 CE),
American author, historian
and philosopher

disposed of the same questions which exercise us."[57]

Emerson introduced Henry David Thoreau (1817-1862 CE), an American author, historian and philosopher, to Indian culture and its shastras. On reading the Vedas and Bhagavad Gitā he said, "What extracts from the Veda I have read fall on me like the light of a higher and purer luminary, which describes a loftier course through a purer stratum."[58] He wrote further, "In the morning I bathe my intellect in the stupendous and cosmogonal philosophy of the Bhagvat Geeta, since

57. *Journals of Ralph Waldo Emerson,* Vol.7, edited by Edward Waldo Emerson and Waldo Emerson Forbes. London: Constable & Co. Ltd., and Boston and New York: Houghton Mifflin Company, 1913, p.511.

58. *The Journal of Henry D. Thoreau,* Vol. II. New York: Dover Publications, Inc. 1962, p.4.

whose composition years of the gods have elapsed, and in comparison with which our modern world and its literature seem puny and trivial."[59]

CONCLUSION

Ancient India produced some of the greatest minds and souls in the world. Their seminal contributions in almost all the fields of human knowledge and experience, both mundane and spiritual, have benefited our world.

India's ancient religion, culture and the advances in all the domains of spirituality and human knowledge were partly learnt, appreciated and spread by many pilgrims, conquerors and scholars from abroad. Some of their testimonies given in this chapter reflect how much they were impressed by the various facets of Hindu religion, culture and science.

SUMMARY

1. Hinduism had a great impact on Egypt, Greece and Rome.

2. Appollonius, a physician, who lived in Turkey during the first century, came to India and learnt yogic techniques and the use of mantras. He profusely praised the people of India.

---

59. *The Writings of Henry David Thoreau,* Vol.II. Boston and New York: Houghton Mifflin and Co. 1906, p.328.

3. Fa-xing, Xuanzang and I-Tsing of China were impressed by the peace, prosperity and noble culture of the Hindus. Hsüan-tsang studied Sanskrit, logic, grammar and philosophy at Nālandā University in Bihar.

4. Al Beruni, an Arab scholar, came to India around 1017 CE and lived for thirteen years. He wrote a voluminous book on Hindu culture and spirituality.

5. Western writers, thinkers and scholars like Mark Twain, Prof. Will Durant, Romain Rolland and others believed India was a cultural millionaire, the mother of Europe's languages and the home for all the dreams of living men.

6. India's ancient scholars and scientists made pioneering discoveries and advances in its social system, medicine, surgery, mathematics, astronomy, architecture, Sanskrit and Vedic literature.

GLOSSARY

A

adhikāra	spiritual eligibility
antaryāmin	inner controller – Paramātmā
aparigraha	non-possession
artha	one of the four human endeavours allowing for the fulfilment of desires for material objects, in particular wealth
asteya	non-stealing
avatāravāda	one of the fundamental beliefs of Hinduism that God manifests on earth in human and other forms to destroy evil and accept the devotion of devotees

B

Bhagavat Geeta	One of the central shastras of Hinduism, consisting of dialogues between Bhagwan Krishna and Arjun on the Mahābhārata battlefield
brahmachāri	celibate
brahmacharya	practice of eight-fold celibacy and being immersed in Brahman (Paramātmā)

C

chit	consciousness

D

dayā	compassion
dharma	righteousness, responsibility, duty

E

ekeshwaravāda	belief in one supreme God

G

guru-shishya	master-disciple

K

kāma	one of the four human endeavours allowing for the regulated fulfilment of one's personal and social desires
kriyamāna	karma or action performed every moment

M

māyā	ignorance, material universe, darkness. One of the five eternal realities. Anything that deviates one from the worship of God
moksha	liberation from *māyā* and cycle of births and deaths, leading to experience of divine bliss
murti	sacred image of God or a deity that is revered and worshipped
murti- pujā	worship of the *murti*

N

nishedhas	prohibitions or don'ts

niyama   moral and spiritual disciplines, and religious codes of conduct prescribed by God, the Satpurush, or the shastras

P

phala pradāta   dispenser of the fruits of one's karmas

prārabdha   portion of one's accumulated karma *(sanchita)* that one is presently experiencing in this birth

preyas   path of sensual pleasure

punarjanma   rebirth

purushārthas   pursuits. Collective term for the four goals legitimately pursued by all Hindus, namely: dharma (duties), *artha* (material wealth), *kāma* (desires), and ultimately, *moksha* (liberation)

R

ruta   cosmic order

S

sampradāya   a tradition handed down from a founder through successive spiritual gurus

satya   truth

shloka   Sanskrit verse

shreyas   path of *moksha*

sthāpatya   style of architecture

V

vairāgya	detachment from material objects and pursuits
varnāshrama	classes and stages of life
vidhi	ritual act. The 'do's' codes of conduct

Y

yama	one of the eight steps in *ashtānga* yoga. Restraint
yantra	'that which holds and protects'. Consecrated geometrical diagram engraved or drawn on metal, paper or palm leaf that represents a deity. Used for worship, protection and control of one's passions